NEWPORT
RHODE ISLAND
The City by the Sea

NEWPORT
RHODE ISLAND

The City by the Sea

SECOND EDITION
REVISED & EXPANDED

TOM GANNON

THE COUNTRYMAN PRESS, INC.
Woodstock, Vermont

No entries for any of the establishments appearing in this book have been solicited or paid for.

Copyright © 1978, 1992 by Tom Gannon
All rights reserved. No part of this book may be reproduced in any form or by any electronic or mechanical means, including information storage and retrieval systems, without permission in writing from the Publisher, except by a reviewer, who may quote brief passages.

The first edition of this book was published in 1978 by the Globe Pequot Press under the title A Guide to Newport Rhode Island (0-87106-097-3)

Library of Congress Cataloging-in-Publication Data

Gannon, Tom, 1944-
Newport, Rhode Island: a guide to the city by the sea/Tom Gannon.—
2nd ed., rev. and expanded.
p. cm.
Rev. ed. of: A guide to Newport, Rhode Island. c1978.
Includes index.
ISBN 0-88150-219-7
1. Newport (R.I.)—Description—Guide-books. I. Gannon, Tom, 1944- Guide to Newport, Rhode Island. II. Title.
F89.N5G15.   1992   91-41017
917.45'70443—dc   CIP

Photographs on the following pages by Tom Gannon: ii, 10, 36, 38, 39, 41, 56, 59, 61, 62, 86, 94, 124, 125, 141, 154, 156, 157.
Photographs on the following pages provided by the Newport County Convention and Visitors Bureau: 30, 34, 49, 51, 68 (Michael Baz).
Cover and book design by Dede Cummings/IPA

Printed in the United States of America
Printed by McNaughton & Gunn
on acid-free, recycled paper

CONTENTS

1. NEWPORT 11
City by the Sea
A Brief History *12*   Newport Today *14*
When to Come *15*   What to Wear *15*   Geography *16*
Getting Here *16*   Getting Oriented *17*   The City *18*
Transportation *20*

2. THINGS TO SEE AND DO 23
Mansions and Major Sights
The Mansions and the Gilded Age *24*
Major Sights *36*

3. MORE TO DO 47
In and around Town
Museums *47*   Churches *53*   Statues *55*
Organized Tours *57*   Area Attractions *58*
Beaches *63*   Special Events *66*   Sports *69*

4. THREE WALKING TOURS 74
Washington Square and Historic Hill *75*
The Point *83*   Victorian Houses *92*

5. OUT OF TOWN TOURS 98
Tiverton and Sakonnet *99*
Fall River *103*   Jamestown *106*

6. WHERE TO STAY 110
Hotels *111*   Inns and Bed-and-Breakfasts *112*
Motels and Motor Lodges *119*   Campgrounds *120*

7. DINING IN NEWPORT   *122*
Four of the Best *124*   Moderate to Expensive *127*
Inexpensive *131*   Pub Food and Sandwiches *132*
Cheap Eats *133*

8. NIGHTLIFE   *135*
Live Music *136*   Dancing *137*   Theater *138*
Movies *138*

9. SHOPPING 140
Art Galleries and Craft Shops *142*   Antiques *143*
Specialty Shops *145*   Clothes *147*   Bookstores *149*

10. IF YOU COME BY SEA   *151*
Getting Here *151*   Moorings and Dockage *155*
Out-of-Town Tie-Ups *158*   Especially for Sail *159*
Sundry Services and Supplies *160*

APPENDIX   *161*
Services, Emergencies and Helpful Phone Numbers
Tourist Information *161*   Health Services *162*
Emergency Numbers *162*   Library *162*
Post Offices *163*

INDEX   *165*

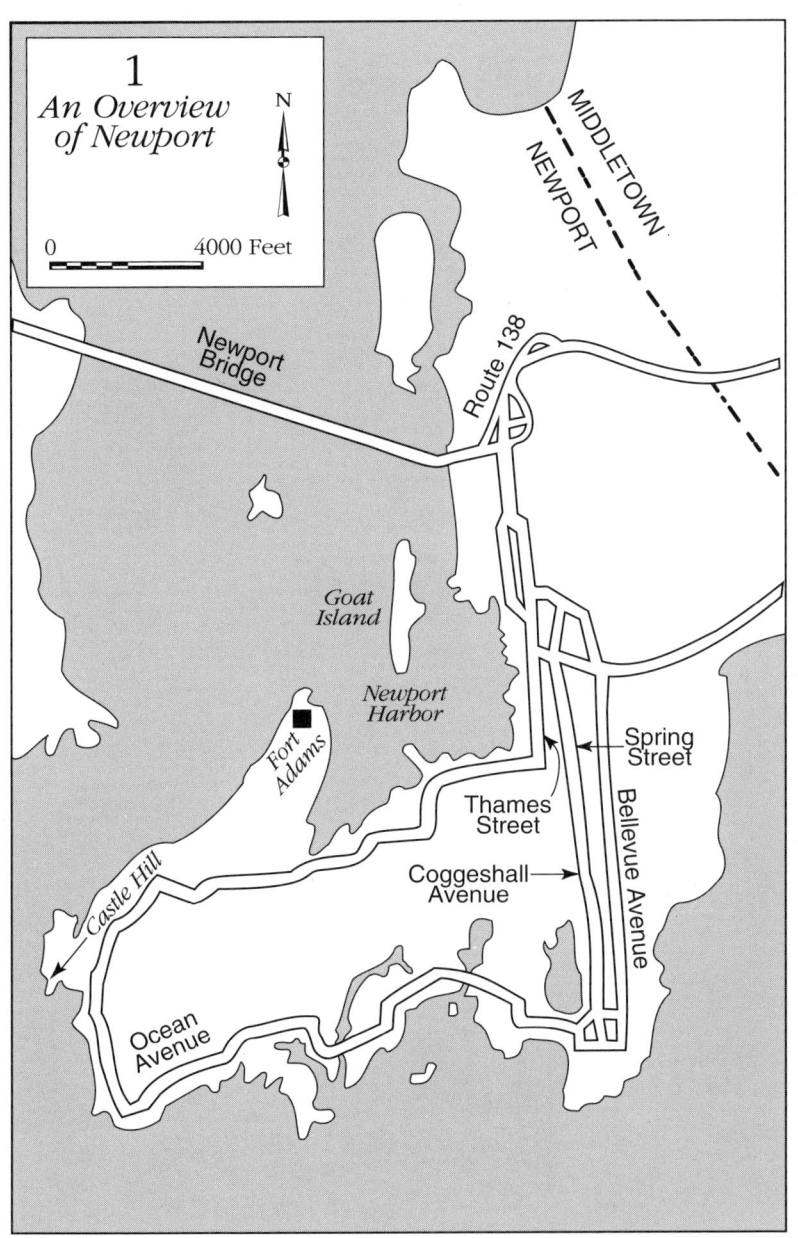

NEWPORT
RHODE ISLAND
The City by the Sea

1
NEWPORT
City by the Sea

෪෪෪෪

LIKE ANCIENT TROY, Thornton Wilder wrote, Newport contains nine cities. Others have counted fewer or more, and everyone has their own ideas of what the cities might be. To the sailor, Newport is a fine deep-water harbor with steady southwest breezes perfect for sailing, as well as host city for some of the world's most prestigious yachting events. To the historian, the colonial neighborhoods represent the most important treasury of eighteenth-century houses in America and are a goldmine of historical events. To the socialite, "America's First Resort," as it is sometimes called, is a reminder of the Gilded Age when society reached its peak, and it is still a summer address second to none. To the music lover, Newport's name is linked forever with the jazz and folk festivals of the fifties and sixties, which continue still, as well as the Newport Music Festival that fills the mansions with classical music for two weeks each summer. To the commercial fisherman—and the grateful seafood consumer—Newport is the lobster capital of the world. To the summer visitor, she is the City by the Sea, with incomparable ocean vistas and soft summer climate.

And to the resident, born and bred or newly arrived, Newport is simply home, a home few would trade for anywhere else.

A Brief History

Newport was founded in the spring of 1639 by a small band of religious refugees from the Massachusetts Bay Colony. Led by William Coddington and John Clarke, the group first settled at the north end of Aquidneck Island (Isle of Peace, to the Wampanoag Indians of the Narragansett tribe); after a winter there they traveled the 15-mile length of the island to the southern tip, where they laid out houses near a spring on land purchased from the Indians for a small amount of money, plus tools and coats.

Because of its excellent harbor and its reputation for religious tolerance, Newport grew rapidly; most of its inhabitants were engaged in trading or some related activity. The city was building ships as early as 1646 and by the middle of the next century was a major port in the New World, rivaling New York in size and importance. Commerce, climate, and culture combined to make Newport a favorite summering place for both Europeans and newly prosperous Americans.

Aided by an exceptionally liberal charter from the ruling British and a local tendency to ignore paying taxes and duties of any kind, colonial Newporters made fortunes in smuggling, privateering (often indistinguishable from outright piracy), and the infamous Triangle Trade, which involved the transportation of molasses, rum, and slaves between the West Indies, Newport, and the west coast of Africa.

The city was no less independent in local politics. When the

Royal Charter of 1644 combined Aquidneck (the "Rhode Island" of Rhode Island) with Providence Plantations, Newport and Providence immediately became competitive, with both claiming to be the capital of the new colony. They compromised by rotating the government seat, but Newport continued to supply most of the governors until the mid-1700s.

Newport's freewheeling economy finally ruffled the heretofore tolerant British, who denounced the government for "conniving with pirates and making Rhode Island their sanctuary." They had a point, for by this time virtually every local merchant had money invested in privateering and a good percentage of the city's male population served on board privateering ships, which ranged the seas from Nova Scotia to Haiti and would as soon plunder a British vessel as one flying the French or Dutch flag. The city was also safe haven for the notorious Captain Kidd, who was captured (and duly executed) only after he'd been lured out of town to Boston. After much resistance, the colonial rulers finally cracked down on piracy; on one occasion, in 1723, they hanged 26 pirates en masse on Long Wharf, noting, however, that the miscreants were "mostly foreigners."

Newporters were not about to give in so easily on the smuggling issue, or to give up trade with the "enemy" French. For much of the eighteenth century the British regularly sent ships to intercept the smuggling and ensure the collection of duties, and the colonists just as regularly chased them out or burned them. Finally, in 1774, the British sent in the frigate HMS *Rose*, which successfully blocked Newport Harbor. The colonists responded by founding the first Continental Navy, and Rhode Island was on its way to declaring independence—which it did, two months before its sister colonies, on May 4, 1776.

The Revolution was to prove costly for Newport. The British landed 6,000 troops in the city on December 7, 1776. During the ensuing three-year occupation, Newport lost much of its population, all of its commerce, and many of its buildings. By war's end, the city was deeply in debt and a poor cousin to the now prospering Providence, which had escaped occupation. The War of 1812 and the development of the railroad ended Newport's hopes of regaining its commercial status through sea trade; instead of becoming the new nation's number one city, it languished for much of the nineteenth century. It wasn't until after the Civil War, when summer visitors rediscovered the city's natural advantages, that any measure of prosperity returned. By the late 1800s, Newport had become a leading summer colony of the rich and was entering its Gilded Age. The foundations were being laid for the city Newport is today.

NEWPORT TODAY

Newport is at once insular and cosmopolitan, a contradiction arising from its being both tucked away on an island and having been a major port for years. Like all port cities, it's been subjected to a wide variety of cultures and ideas from around the world. Much of this influence took hold, so it is no surprise that the grandiose mansions are patterned after the great houses of Europe, that many of the homes and antique stores are filled with china from the China Trade, and that, with the exception of seafood, the main cuisine is French.

Then again, as on all islands, there remains a detachment from the mainland. Newport has little in common with the rest of New England, or Rhode Island, for that matter. Many Newporters have not traveled widely—the 35-mile trip to Providence is looked upon as a major excursion. Some boast of never having left the island at all.

But these are the natives. Besides those who have lived here for generations, there are many who came either via the navy, as tourists or sailors, or for a special event like the America's Cup or Jazz Festival, and decided this was the place they wanted to live. Among the new arrivals are a good number of craftsmen, artists, and writers who like the relative quiet of a small city coupled with proximity to New York and Boston.

The result has been a lively mix of population that makes Newport both conservative and liberal, traditional and innovative, closed in upon itself and open to anyone.

WHEN TO COME

Newport, with its renewed interest in tourism, is increasingly becoming a 12-month town. Most of the activity revolves around the summer months when sailing events, concerts, and outdoor fairs abound. These are the busiest months— rooms often are hard to find and prices are at their peak. Spring and fall are the best bets—you'll find Newport less hurried but still at its finest. In winter, the best month is December, when the city celebrates Christmas in Newport, a revival of the noncommercial observance of the holiday. Houses are decorated with clear bulb candles and natural greens, special events are scheduled virtually every day, and visitor and resident alike can get a sense of how Christmas was celebrated in colonial times. January and February are probably the least desirable times to visit the city. It's cold, the streets are quiet at night, and many of the better restaurants have closed for a month or two of vacation.

WHAT TO WEAR

Despite Newport's reputation as a chic watering spot for the rich and privileged, Newporters are surprisingly casual about their dress habits. You'll need a jacket and tie for some of the better restaurants or special Newport Music Festival concerts, for example, but for virtually everything else the word is informal. During the daytime, shorts or jeans and T-shirts are almost a Newport uniform; it seems as if as many T-shirts are sold here as anywhere. Many of the nightclubs frown upon them, however, and won't let you in unless you dress up a bit. Bathing suits are rarely seen except close to the beach and on or around boats.

Newport is a walking city, so wear something comfortable on your feet. Visitors should also bring along a sweater and/or windbreaker regardless of the season. Even during the warmest months, cool onshore breezes at night bring the temperature down. Some form of rain protection is a good idea, too, especially in the fall and spring, the rainy seasons. In winter, the ever-present winds from the north warrant the warmest clothes you can pack. The temperature may not be that low, but the chill factor makes heavy jackets, hats, and gloves necessary most days.

GEOGRAPHY

Newport is a surprisingly tiny city, with a population of about 30,000 living within 7.7 square miles. The city is situated on the southernmost point of Aquidneck Island, which is 15 miles long and about four miles across at Newport. To the west, Newport is connected to Jamestown, another island, by the Newport Bridge. Jamestown, in turn, is connected to mainland Rhode Island by the Jamestown Bridge. Newport's neighbors to the north are Middletown, which has a population somewhat less than Newport, and Portsmouth, the largest town on the island in area but smallest in population. The northern end of the island is connected to mainland Bristol by the Mount Hope Bridge, and to mainland Tiverton by the Sakonnet River Bridge.

GETTING HERE

Newport is not yet linked directly to any major highways, although plans are afoot to make it a stopping point on one great interstate running through New England to Cape Cod. You can, however, get close to Newport by highway and consider the rest of the trip the scenic route. From the west, in the general direction of New York and Connecticut, the best route is I-95. From I-95, you can get off at RI 138, which leads you through rural Rhode Island, over the Jamestown Bridge, and on into Newport. The Jamestown Bridge is free, but there's a $2 toll for passenger cars crossing the Newport Bridge. From I-95, you can also pick up US 1 in Westerly, Rhode Island, just over the Connecticut border, and follow this or scenic RI 1A through Southern Rhode Island to the Jamestown Bridge. From the north, Newport is linked with RI 114 and 138. RI 138 ties into I-195, which passes through Providence; this route eventually hooks up with RI 24, which leads to Boston or the Cape. The nearest train depots are off RI 138 in Kingston, Rhode Island, and in Providence, where bus links will get you (eventually) to Newport. Those wishing to rent a car might want to leave the train at the first Rhode Island stop in Westerly. Be sure to check train schedules; not all commuter trains from New York make the Kingston stop.

The nearest sizable airport is T.F. Green Airport in Warwick, Rhode Island, where you can rent a car, connect with a shuttle van to Newport ($13 each way) or hop a commuter flight to the small state airport in Middletown. Airport shuttles are operated by Cozy Cab until midnight each day. It's best to make a reservation if you know your time of arrival. You can reach Cozy Cab at 401-846-2500. (Note: the area code for all Rhode Island is 401.)

Getting Oriented

For anyone unfamiliar with Newport, the best place to start is the Gateway Center at 23 America's Cup Avenue, operated by the Newport Tourism and Convention Authority (401-849-8098). The building is located near the waterfront, just north of Long Wharf and one block west of Washington Square. Gateway visitors receive one-half hour of free parking in the garage behind the center, or you can park free on one of the neighboring streets.

Inside the center, you'll find an aerial map display of Newport and its various attractions; several ongoing videos, including a 16-screen presentation of the city's highlights; hundreds of brochures touting different hotels and inns, restaurants and services, and a small gift shop. There are several information booths staffed by knowledgeable and helpful personnel. Above the main information booth there are several monitors that offer information about room availability and provide phone numbers of hotels, inns and bed-and-breakfasts. If you haven't made room reservations ahead of time, this is the place to start. There are a number of dedicated free phone lines that will put you in direct touch with participating hotels and inns.

The Gateway is also the starting point for several tours, including Viking Tours, the city's oldest tour firm, and the Viking trolley, which provides basic transportation—no narration—around town. Tickets to various services and attractions can be bought here.

Bonanza Bus has a station and waiting room in an annex to the center. Outside under the canopy, Bonanza buses and Rhode Island Public Transit Authority buses can be boarded.

THE CITY

Newport is designed for walking. Once you are within the general area of downtown, you can walk to just about everything—stores, restaurants, nightclubs, and historical attractions. During the summer, when narrow colonial streets and an overabundance of vehicles make driving almost impossible, walking is the quickest and least frustrating way to get around. The Gateway Center is a block west of Washington Square, the heart of the old city. The square runs into Thames Street, which in turn loops into America's Cup Avenue for a stretch along the waterfront, then continues on its own southward. This area of about

12 blocks is the main commercial district and the heart of the city's nightlife. The other main business district is on Bellevue Avenue, a reasonable walk from Thames Street, but uphill, so you might want to take your car after a day of sightseeing. The three main identifiable neighborhoods are Historic Hill, which extends up from Thames Street to Bellevue Avenue; the Point, which lies between Upper Thames and the harbor (behind the Gateway Center), and Lower Thames, or the Fifth Ward, toward the southern end of the harbor. Much of the land at the southern tip of Newport is unpopulated, a legacy from the days of the large estates. There has been some private development in recent years, but much of the land has been set aside to preserve the natural beauty of the area bordering Ocean Drive.

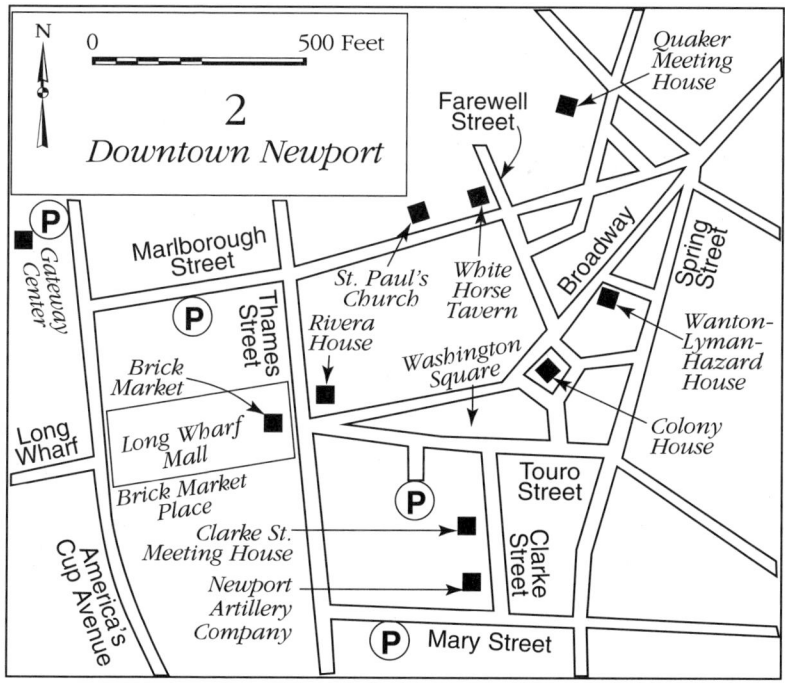

TRANSPORTATION

By Car—Traveling around Newport by car can be difficult, especially during the busy summer months. Expect to move slowly and spend a lot of time backed up at traffic signals. Weekends and holidays are the worst, with many regional day-trippers adding to the congestion. Because of the preponderance of drivers unfamiliar with the city, motorists should stay alert, for example checking both ways at intersections, even one-way streets. Remember that pedestrians have the right of way in crosswalks. Also beware of bicyclists (illegally) moving against traffic on one-way streets.

Parking at the side of the street is free, but there is a two-hour limit, diligently enforced on major thoroughfares by traffic patrollers who chalk your tires. Also watch for signs that denote areas of restricted sticker parking; from May to October from 6 p.m., these are for residents only, although many inns and guest houses will have a "guest" sticker you can borrow. Municipal parking is scanty, but a better bargain than most private lots. The main city lot is downtown off Thames Street between Mary and Church streets. A second, smaller lot off Touro Street in Washington Square offers limited free parking. Some commercial lots, notably the ones at Long Wharf Mall at the foot of Washington Square and the adjoining Brick Market Place shopping area, offer validated parking. The lot and garage behind the Gateway Center, close to most downtown destinations and the historical Point area, have room for about 500 cars.

By Bus—The Rhode Island Public Transit Authority (847-0209) operates regular commuter bus service throughout the city and to nearby Middletown. Stops include major shopping centers and the beaches. Fare is 75 cents, exact change; transfers cost 15 cents. Transit Authority buses to Providence, Jamestown, and the train station at Kingston depart from the Gateway Center; the private Bonanza bus line (846-1820), which offers service to

Massachusetts and Boston, has a station and waiting room at the Gateway Center.

By Trolley—Green, red, and blue trolleys operated by Viking Tours make continuous loops through the center of town and out to the mansions on Bellevue Avenue, from 10 a.m. to 4 p.m. Tickets, which can be purchased at the Gateway Center, cost $7.50 for adults, $3.50 for kids and are good for one day's worth of unlimited rides.

By Taxi—Cozy Cab (846-2500) is the largest taxi service in the city. The initial charge is $1.40, good for one-sixth of a mile, with 20 cents per sixth of a mile thereafter. Yellow Cab (846-1500) is owned by the same firm and has the same rates. ABC Taxi (846-7200) charges an initial fee of $1.20 and then charges 20 cents at increments of one-eighth of a mile. The yellow-painted Cozy and Yellow cabs and the gold-toned ABC cabs can usually be found in Washington Square or near the Gateway Center.

By Bicycle—Ten Speed Spokes, (847-5609), 18 Elm Street, off America's Cup Avenue, Newport's oldest leasing firm, has hourly to weekly bike rentals. Because of Newport's hills, we'd skip the one-speed and take the ten. Locks are available on request.

Block Island Ferry—A memorable ocean trip to Block Island, about 24 miles offshore, leaves from the state pier at Fort Adams at 10:30 a.m. daily and returns about 5 p.m. The season runs from June 22 to Labor Day weekend. Fare is $8.50 for same-day round trip. No cars, passengers only. For information (in-season) call 849-7712, or you can reach the ferry company, Interstate Navigation, in New London, Connecticut, at 203-442-7891.

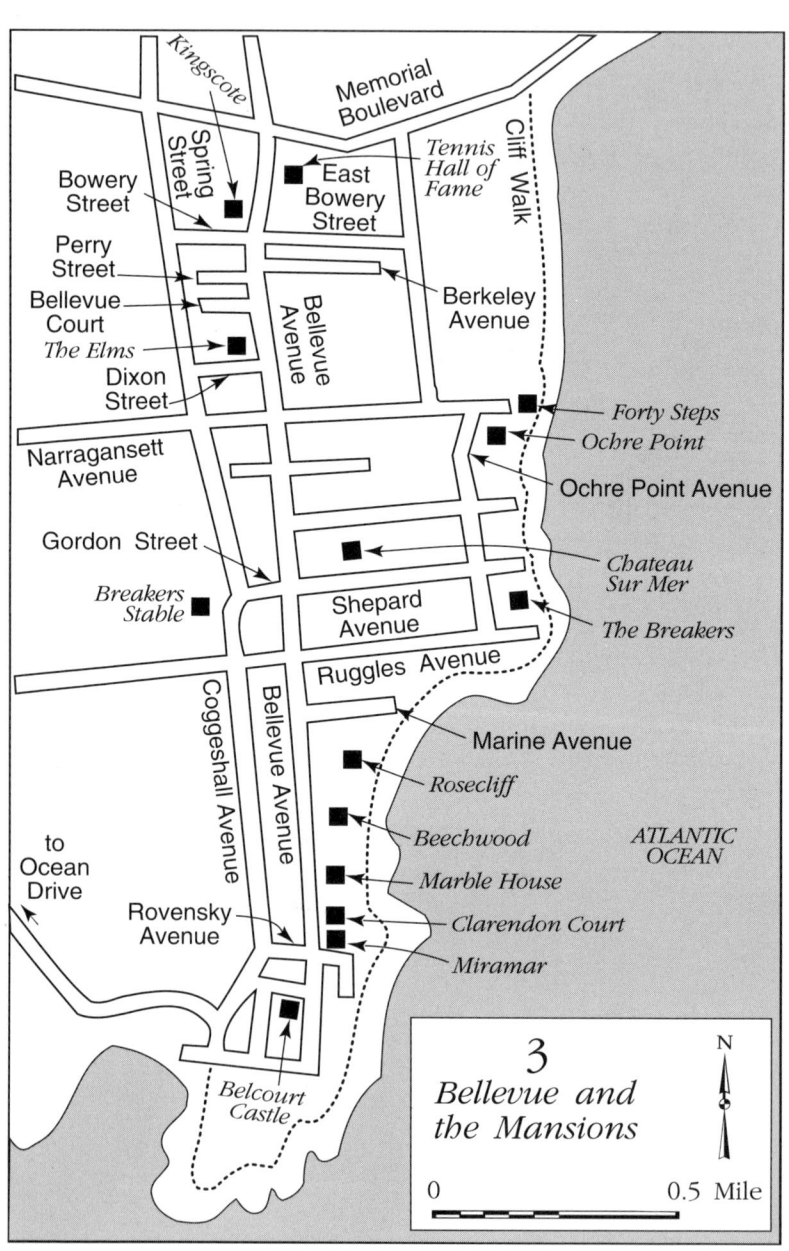

3
Bellevue and the Mansions

2
THINGS TO SEE AND DO
Mansions and Major Sights

🙢🙢🙢🙢

MUCH OF WHAT THERE IS TO DO in Newport is connected with its history—which isn't as dull as it may sound. In some cities if you want to see history, you have to go to a museum. In Newport, you just take a right or left out of your hotel and start walking. There is a handful of museums in Newport, and the mansions technically could be considered museums. But most of the city's history has been incorporated into contemporary life—in the eighteenth-century dwellings that serve as homes, shops or restaurants, and in the narrow gas-lit lanes.

Out in the open air you'll also have a chance to enjoy Newport's natural beauty, an attribute even the natives never seem to tire of. There's the Ocean Drive, the Cliff Walk, and a number of conveniently located seaside parks. Beyond it all is the sea; you can experience the magnificent waves breaking over the rocks at the southern tip, the vista of First and Second beaches from the heights of Memorial Boulevard, or the quiet of the inner harbor. Be sure to catch as many sunsets as you can—Newport Harbor conveniently looks to the west. There are also the regular events that go on in the city, especially during summer and early fall (see Chapter 3, "Special Events").

THE MANSIONS AND THE GILDED AGE

Henry James called them "white elephants" and "grotesque." A former French ambassador—perhaps forgetting—Versailles, once referred to them as "horrors." Others have described them as the perfect symbols of the Gilded Age, a time when America's newly rich sought ways to flaunt their tax-free wealth. Architectural monstrosities or gracious reminders of a past glory, the mansions that line Bellevue Avenue and Ocean Drive are without a doubt the single most popular attraction in the City by the Sea. They are visited by more than one million people each year, and to come to Newport without seeing at least one would be like missing the sea.

Newport was a favorite summer place for the wealthy since well before the Revolution, but it wasn't until the 1880s, when New York society began arriving in force, that the city entered its heyday. Much of the opulence—some would say extravagance—of the time was due to a new definition of "wealth." Where once the accumulation of a million dollars defined wealth, the new fortunes, built on coal, railroads, oil, and finance, were measured in tens and hundreds of millions. Lacking hereditary titles or long family tradition, the members of this new elite attempted to create an instant American aristocracy by doing what they did best—spend money. They spent it on dazzling gold-encrusted carriages with imported English thoroughbreds to pull them. They spent it on jewelry and wardrobes—the well-dressed woman sported 80 or 90 dresses a season, one for every occasion. Mrs. Henry Clews, the best of the well dressed, was said to set aside $10,000 each summer for "mistakes" in her wardrobe.

The Golden Era was ushered in with lavish balls and dinners, set in equally lavish surroundings. No matter that a family might spend no more than a month here in the summer—each "summer cottage" had to be more opulent than the one next door. And opulent they were. The Marble House, including furnishings, cost a total of $11 million when it was built in 1892, about a tenth of what it would cost today. Not so much, really, when you consider that families spent as much as $200,000 for a single party. For her Fête des Roses in 1902, Grace Vanderbilt not only provided $10,000 worth of "favors" for her guests, for their diversion she had the entire company of the hit play, "The Wild Rose," transported from New York, a feat that involved closing the theater in New York for two days.

The summer colonists spent so much and so freely that a newspaper correspondent was prompted to report that Newport's rich "devoted themselves to pleasure regardless of expense." Not so, corrected Colonel George Waring, a prominent resident, who explained the rich were actually devoting themselves to expense regardless of pleasure. A disapproving Henry James wrote that the summer visitors "danced and they drove and they rode, they dined and wined and dressed and flirted and yachted and Casino'd." It couldn't last, of course, and increasing taxes and finally the Depression put an end to the excesses of America's richest families. The great summer houses became too much to afford, and by 1950 only a handful were left in private hands. Fortunately for posterity, the Preservation Society of Newport County, formed in 1945 to preserve the historic colonial-era Hunter House, began acquiring the mansions as they closed up and now has six of the best, including Rosecliff, The Elms and The Breakers.

A word about the architecture of the mansions and Richard Morris Hunt, who designed some of the great ones. Most of the architecture is derivative, modeled after the great houses and palaces of Europe. The European tradition came naturally to Hunt, who was the first American to receive a degree from the Ecole des Beaux-Arts in Paris, where he became familiar with the neoclassical and neobaroque design elements regarded as the height of artistic expression. His training came in handy for an America that after the Civil War had no defined style of its own and was compelled to look back to Europe for direction. After spending the years 1843 to 1854 in Europe, Hunt returned to the United States, where he worked on the Capitol Building in Washington, the base of the Statue of Liberty, and the Fogg Museum at Harvard. He spent the last ten years of his life designing some of the best-known mansions on Bellevue Avenue, including The Breakers and Marble House, as well as the Biltmore House in Asheville, North Carolina. Hunt died in Newport on July 31, 1895.

All of the mansions open to the public are either on or directly off Bellevue Avenue between Bowery Street and the beginning of Ocean Drive. The Preservation Society houses are well marked with green and white signs, and free parking is provided at each estate. Tours generally last about 45 minutes.

Kingscote, on Bellevue Avenue at the corner of Bowery Street, is the first mansion you come to heading south down the avenue, but perhaps it should be saved until several of the other mansions have been seen. After visiting the huge granite and marble structures farther along, Kingscote, with its wooden exterior and charming early Victorian design, comes as a welcome change of pace. Among the oldest summer residences in the city, Kingscote was built in 1839 by Richard Upjohn for George Noble Jones of Savannah, Georgia, who continued the pre-Civil War tradition of southern families summering in Newport. On what was, at the time, two acres surrounded mostly by farmland, Upjohn designed a Gothic Revival house that was picturesque without being overly quaint. A dining room was added in 1881 by Stanford White of McKim, Mead and White, who later designed Rosecliff.

The least well known of the Society's houses, Kingscote is well worth a visit to see its early Rhode Island furniture and art. There is also a priceless collection of porcelain and paintings courtesy of later owner William Henry King, who had been engaged in the China Trade. The interior of the house is rich with parquet floors, a Tiffany glass wall in the dining room, and mahogany paneling.

Kingscote is open 10 a.m. to 5 p.m. daily from late April to the end of September, weekends in spring and fall. Cost of admission is $6 for adults and $3 for children ages 6 to 11, less if a combination ticket to more than one house is purchased. For information call 847-1000.

The Elms on Bellevue Avenue, a block or so south of Kingscote, is a favorite of those who know the mansions well. Built in 1901 for Philadelphia coal baron Edward J. Berwind, the French-style chateau is the best furnished of the Society's houses. As attractive as the house is—in a coolly classical manner—the biggest attraction is the 14 acres of grounds and sunken French gardens complete with terraces, fountains, statues and teahouses. There's a wide variety of exotic trees and shrubs, all labeled. This is a perfect place to stroll on a sunny afternoon.

Designed by Horace Trumbauer of Philadelphia after the eighteenth-century Chateau d'Asnieres near Paris, The Elms offers more than meets the eye. Although, from the ground, it appears to be a two-story structure topped with a sculpture-bearing parapet, in reality there is a hidden third story that contains the servants' quarters—sixteen rooms and three baths. In the same way, kitchen and laundry facilities are discreetly concealed in the basement. A secret underground railroad, which surfaced a block away on Dixon Street, transported the coal that fueled the huge burners that kept house and furnishings warm during winter.

The Elms is open daily from 10 a.m. to 5 p.m. from April through September, weekends in spring and fall. Admission is

$6, $3 for children; less with a combination ticket. For information call 847-1000.

Chateau-Sur-Mer on Bellevue, to the left, is a fine example of mid-Victorian architecture and one of the older mansions in Newport. It's actually a blending of two structures, the first built in 1852 by a local contractor for William Shepard Wetmore, another China Trader who settled in Newport. Twenty years later, it was enlarged by Richard Morris Hunt, best known at the time for his stick style Victorian cottages. Hunt added a French ballroom and so altered the house that what you see today is largely his design. Some critics felt he converted a charming Victorian villa into a somewhat severe pile of granite, but the imposing result was a hint of grander summer palaces to come.

The neighborhood surrounding Chateau-Sur-Mer is built up now, but once the 35-acre estate offered a clear view of the sea, hence its name. Note the many exotic plants on the grounds and the Chinese moon gate on the south side, which once framed an ocean vista.

The first room on the tour is the elegantly paneled library, originally the kitchen. Once it served as a billiard parlor for the second owner, George Peabody Wetmore, governor and senator, but when he died his spinster daughters had the pool table removed and the cue racks converted to coat racks. The house is notable for its extensive wood paneling done in the "honest" style—all the mistakes were left to be seen—and large ornate mirrors. Many of the original furnishings can be seen, including a fine collection of Rose Medallion and Rose Mandarin china sets collected by Wetmore. On the second floor is a special treat for children—a charming collection of Victorian toys and dollhouses. Each Christmas, the Preservation Society decorates the house in Victorian holiday style and opens it to the public.

Chateau-Sur-Mer is open daily from 10 a.m. to 5 p.m. April through September, weekends in spring and fall. Admission is $6, $3 for children; less with a combination ticket. For information call 847-1000.

Things to See and Do

The Breakers on Ochre Point Avenue is the largest, most opulent and best known of the Newport mansions. To reach it, turn off Bellevue Avenue at either Victoria, Shepard or Ruggles avenues. The estate is enclosed by a beautiful, ornamental, wrought iron gate. In back, the grounds command an awe-inspiring view of the Atlantic Ocean. The grounds also feature an original parterre garden and many unusual imported trees and shrubs.

Covering nearly an acre of Cornelius Vanderbilt's 11-acre oceanfront property, the four-story limestone palace contains 70 rooms including a two-story ballroom that epitomizes the Gilded Age. It took a force of hundreds of workers just two years to complete the building. Entire rooms were built overseas by European craftsmen and shipped to Newport. Crystal chandeliers were equipped for gas as well as electricity in case the power failed. Bathroom taps supplied either fresh rainwater or salt water, hot and cold. The house contains all original furnishings.

The Breakers was opened with a coming-out party for 20-year-old Gertrude Vanderbilt on an August evening in 1895. Missing was its architect Richard Hunt, who had died on July 31. Cornelius Vanderbilt, who inherited $70 million of the Vanderbilt family's railroad empire fortune, was not able to enjoy his summer home for long; he suffered a stroke in 1896 and died three years later at the age of fifty-six. The Countess Laszlo Scechenyi (née Gladys Vanderbilt) sold the house to the Preservation Society in 1972. Countess Szapary, her daughter, still resides in the family quarters on the third floor.

The Breakers is open daily from 10 a.m. to 5 p.m. from early April through September. During summer, the mansion stays open until 8 p.m. on Fridays, Saturdays and Sundays. Admission is $7.50, $3.50 for children; less with a combination ticket. 847-6543.

Breakers Stable/Carriage House, Coggeshall Avenue. Built in 1895 by Cornelius Vanderbilt, the stable contains a central

The east side of the Breakers, facing the ocean, features double loggias (arcades) that served as summer porches.

carriage room on the ground floor and 28 stalls at the rear. The horses are gone, but some period carriages and coaches are on display. Open daily from late April through September. Admission is $3, $2 for children, and $2 if you display a ticket stub from one of the Preservation Society mansions.

Ochre Court on Ochre Point Avenue now serves as the administration building for Salve Regina College. It was designed in 1891 by Richard Hunt for Ogden Goelet, a wealthy New York real estate developer. The magnificent 50-room summer home was modeled by Hunt after the medieval chateaux of France's Loire Valley.

While much of the building is now taken up by college offices, visitors can see the great hall, which rises three stories. In keeping with the medieval atmosphere, the walls are finished with heraldic designs carved in Caen stone. Many of the original furnishings have been removed, but the hall still has the huge marble Atlas table, so-called because of the carved Atlas figures which support it. Made of Brescia marble, the table takes fifteen men to move. Other rooms open to the public contain many fine period paintings, and there is a stained glass window dating back to the late Middle Ages above the stair landing on the grand staircase. Outside, the grounds sweep down to the Cliff Walk and a beautiful view of the ocean.

Ochre Court is open daily from 9 a.m. to 4 p.m. Admission is free but donations are welcome.

Rosecliff on Bellevue Avenue is possibly the most romantic-looking mansion, designed in 1900 by Stanford White to resemble the Grand Trianon at Versailles. With its white terra-cotta finish, heart-shaped grand staircase, and beautiful rose gardens, it's no wonder Hollywood chose it to be the home of Jay Gatsby (as played by Robert Redford) in its 1974 film version of *The Great Gatsby*.

With the largest ballroom of any Newport mansion, Rosecliff was perfect for the brilliant entertainments favored by society during the Gilded Age. Mrs. Hermann Oelrichs, wife of the first owner, gave a party that is still remembered in society annals. Dubbed "The White Ball," the party required all the women guests to come dressed in white and to powder their hair. The men, for contrast, wore black. The ballroom was completely adorned with white roses, orchids, and lillies of the valley, and "Tessie" Oelrichs even had constructed a fleet of full-size artificial white ships that was anchored out back in the Atlantic and illuminated for full effect. (Bellevue Avenue wasn't all-powerful—the local naval commander declined to put his White Fleet at Tessie's disposal for the ball.) The mistress of the house, the daughter of an Irish immigrant who struck it rich in the California Gold Rush, was equally demanding when it came to housecleaning: every bed was made anew each day, and when Mrs. Oelrichs traveled to hotels, she brought her own bedding with her.

Like many romantic settings, Rosecliff saw its share of tragedy. A later owner had the mansion renovated for his family without ever being able to visit it, for on the way to view the finished work, he was killed in a car accident nearby. The family immediately sold the house.

Rosecliff is open daily from 10 a.m. to 5 p.m. from early April through September. Admission is $6, $3 for children; less with a combination ticket. For information call 847-1000.

Beechwood, the stuccoed brick mansion to the south of Rosecliff on Bellevue, was designed by Calvert Vaux and Andrew Jackson Downing and built in 1851–52. (Vaux was the less famous partner of landscape artist Frederick Law Olmstead, who designed Central and Prospect parks in New York City.) With its high-ceilinged piazzas on three sides, Beechwood was a Newport showcase for years. But it wasn't until the 1880s when Mrs. William Backhouse Astor, "Queen of the Four Hundred," took up residence that Beechwood came into its own.

Caroline Astor, who married the grandson of John Jacob Astor I, was the ruling grande dame of New York's Fifth Avenue society. By her own definition, the family she married into was "old money," unlike the Vanderbilts who had made their money in "trade" and whom, for a time, she was able to bar from the inner circles of society. According to Ward McAllister, Mrs. Astor's minion and self-appointed social arbiter, the term "Four Hundred" referred to the number of persons who could comfortably fit into the Astor's New York ballroom. "If you go outside that number, you strike people who are either not at ease in a ballroom or else make other people not at ease."

Mrs. Astor presided over her dinners at Beechwood regally and was noted for her diamond wearing proclivities—she wore a diamond tiara over her black pompadour complemented by a three-strand diamond necklace of 204 stones. Her son, John Jacob Astor IV, was one of many society figures to go down with the *Titanic* on its maiden voyage.

House tours are conducted by costumed guides who greet you as one of Mrs. Astor's guests and provide lively and humorous sketches of life at the time during 45-minute tours. Beechwood is open daily from 10 a.m. to 5 p.m. from mid-May through September, from 10 a.m. to 4 p.m. Fridays, Saturdays, and Sundays in off-season. Admission is $7 for adults, $5.50 for children. For information call 846-3772.

Marble House on Bellevue Avenue just past Beechwood really looks like a mansion, with its white marble driveway which curves up to an arch under the porte cochere at the front entrance, its pillasters and capitals, and its ten tons of bronzed entrance grille. Designed in 1892 by Richard Hunt for William K. Vanderbilt, the Marble House was modeled after the Petit Trianon at Versailles, Marie Antoinette's private hideaway. It remains one of Newport's most sumptuous structures and epitomizes Hunt's ideas of the beaux-arts neoclassical style. Like The Breakers, the house retains it original furnishings—which cost a total of $9 million back at the turn of the century.

Out on the grounds, Alva Vanderbilt oversaw the construction of a red-and-gold lacquered Chinese teahouse. When she realized there was no means of making tea in it, she had a tiny railroad built from the main house which carried her footmen back and forth with a silver tea service.

The Gold Ballroom—the gold is real—was the scene of many extravagant entertainments. It was here that Alva (as Mrs. Oliver Hazard Perry Belmont—she had divorced William Vanderbilt and married her neighbor) conducted one of her most famous dinners—ten courses at which the one hundred "guests" were dogs in various forms of fancy dress. The dogs dined at the table on such delicacies as stewed liver and rice and shredded dog biscuits. The newly divorced Mrs. Vanderbilt had given a more serious entertainment earlier, in 1895, to present her (unwilling) 18-year-old daughter, Consuelo, to the titled, but poor, Duke of Marlborough, who dutifully proposed. After an unhappy marriage, Consuelo divorced the duke in 1921 to marry again, for love.

Marble House, the last of the Preservation Society houses along Bellevue, is open daily from 10 a.m. to 5 p.m. from early

April through September. Open summer months until 8 p.m. on Wednesdays and Thursdays. Admission is $6, $3 for children; less with a combination ticket. For information call 847-1000.

Belcourt Castle at Bellevue and Lakeview avenues near the start of Ocean Drive is a museum-castle owned by the Howard B. Tinney family. Richard Hunt designed it for Oliver Hazard Perry Belmont in 1891, based on plans from the Louis XIII hunting lodge he saw in France. Though built at the height of Hunt's career, Belcourt is more medieval-looking and less in the grand style than his better-known palaces across the Avenue.

Belcourt Castle contains 60 rooms, each done in a different period of French, Italian or English design. Notable features include the hand-carved Grand Stair, a reproduction of the Francis I stair in the Musée de Cluny in Paris, and the elegant Versailles dining room. Within the many rooms is the Tinney family collection of antiques and art treasures from 32 countries, valued at $3 million. The castle contains many fine Oriental rugs and what is said to be the largest private collection of stained glass in the country. The Tinneys also display a 23-karat gold Royal Coronation coach, decorated with oil paintings and gold lead and weighing four tons.

One of the nicest features of the castle is the center courtyard where Mr. Belmont had his horses exercised daily (the stables are built into the house). Mr. Belmont was kind to his horses: they slept in a Hunt-designed stable on white linen sheets embroidered with the Belmont crest. After a tour by guides in medieval costume, visitors are invited to have tea or coffee.

Belcourt Castle is open daily from 10 a.m. to 5 p.m. June through September, from 10 a.m. to 4 p.m. during spring and fall, and weekends only in winter. Admission is $6 for adults ($5 for seniors), $3.50 for students, and $2 for children ages 6-12. For information call 846-0669.

Alva Vanderbilt's Chinese teahouse on the grounds of Marble House, overlooking the Cliff Walk.

Colony House, Washington Square.

MAJOR SIGHTS

Colony House, at the head of Washington Square. This handsome building, designed by Richard Munday and built in 1739–41, is the second oldest capitol building in the United States. It served as the seat of government for both the colony and the State of Rhode Island when Newport was the capital city. Colony House once was the site of public whippings and pillorying of colonial lawbreakers. (Law in the colonies was harsh; children who struck their parents, for example, could be put to death.) It also played a central role in the Revolution. It was from here that Governor Stephen Hopkins issued the orders in July 1764 to open fire on the British warship *St. John*—possibly the first shots fired in what was to become the Revolutionary

War. And it was from here that Rhode Island declared its independence from Britain on May 4, 1776, anticipating the Declaration of Independence by two months. During the war George Washington met here with French general Rochambeau to plan the final defeat of Cornwallis at Yorktown. Other notables who have been entertained at the Colony House include Lafayette and presidents Jefferson, Jackson and Eisenhower. Upstairs, in the Governor's Council Chamber, hangs a full-length portrait of Washington by Gilbert Stuart.

The Colony House is open for free tours daily from July to Labor Day, 9:30 a.m. to 4 p.m., and by appointment during off-season. For information call 846-2980.

Touro Synagogue, 72 Touro Street, is the oldest house of Jewish worship in North America and a National Historic Site. Jews had been coming to Newport since the mid-seventeenth century, encouraged by Rhode Island's tolerance of all forms of religion. After more than one hundred years of worshipping in private homes, the Jewish community, under the leadership of Isaac de Touro, commissioned noted colonial architect Peter Harrison in 1759 to build a synagogue. At the time, there were an estimated 15 Jewish families in Newport, many of Spanish or Portuguese Sephardic origin. Harrison, using descriptions of synagogues in Portugal and Holland and designs by English architect Inigo Jones, created a simple but classical building whose lines may have influenced Thomas Jefferson's plans for Monticello.

It was to the Jewish community here that George Washington pledged religious freedom without restraint in the nation newly freed from Britain. The proclamation, containing the stirring lines, "To bigotry no sanction, to persecution no assistance . . ." is read at the synagogue each year. After the Revolution, Touro served as a meeting place for the General Assembly and the state Supreme Court while the Colony House was being repaired. The interior, one of the most beautiful in colonial houses of worship, has been restored to its original condition. Among the many treasures here is a Scroll of Laws dating from 1658.

Touro Synagogue is open June to Labor Day, Monday to Friday from 10 a.m. to 5 p.m. and Sundays from 10-5. Spring and fall hours are Fridays and Sundays from 1–3 p.m. Open winter Sundays from 1–3, and by appointment. Saturday services at 9 a.m. Friday services at 7:30 p.m. in summer, 6 p.m. the rest of the year. For information call 847-4794.

A short walk up the street is Touro Cemetery, at the corner of Bellevue Avenue and Kay Street, which dates from the 1640s. You'll find headstones here with inscriptions in Hebrew, Spanish, Portuguese, and English. Open daily.

Touro Synagogue.

Things to See and Do

The Old Stone Mill, Touro Park at the corner of Mill Street and Bellevue Avenue. One of the real architectural oddities in America, the stone mill has been attributed to the Vikings, the Indians, the Portuguese, and English colonists. The best guesses place it somewhere between 1100 and 1650. Although recent thinking holds it was built as a windmill by Governor Benedict Arnold, fifth great-grandfather of the notorious Arnold, the peculiar architecture, along with the suit of armor found farther up the coast and immortalized in Longfellow's "The Skeleton in Armor," has convinced many locals the Vikings were responsible. Some guess it may have served as a lighthouse, while others maintain it was simply Arnold's mill-grainery, fortified

The Old Stone Mill, one of the real architectural oddities in America. In Touro Park off Bellevue Avenue.

because of the ongoing Indian Wars. At any rate, situated as it is in the midst of one of New-port's prettiest parks, it is worth a visit. If you hang around long enough, you'll probably hear a new theory about it.

A short walk down bordering Pelham Street is a tiny historical cemetery where Arnold is buried.

Trinity Church, a National Historic Landmark on the corner of Church and Spring streets at the head of Queen Anne Square is the finest church building in Newport and possibly all of America. Trinity Church was built in 1725–26 by Richard Munday after designs by Christopher Wren, the great seventeenth-century English architect. What's especially remarkable is that Munday chose to interpret English baroque principles using wood rather than masonry.

The church was spared British depravation during the Revolution because of its Church of England ties. Today it is notable for its tall, graceful spire, its Tiffany stained glass windows (the first two on the left), and its triple-deck wineglass pulpit, the only one in America. Distinguished visitors have included George Washington (his pew was No. 81) and Dean George Berkeley, later bishop of Cloyne, who often preached here during his three-year stay. More recently, the Archbishop of Canterbury and Queen Elizabeth II visited in 1976 as part of the Bicentennial celebration. The gallery holds the original organ case given to the church in 1733 by Berkeley; it was made by Richard Bridge of London, is believed to have been played by Handel, and is the second oldest organ in the country.

In the small graveyard beside the church lies Lucia, the infant daughter of Berkeley, as well as Admiral d'Arsac de Ternay, whose fleet arrived with Rochambeau during the Revolution and who died here of fever. A monument to de Ternay, given by King Louis XVI, is in the church vestibule.

Trinity underwent extensive restoration in 1987 after surveyors, investigating the cause of chronically peeling paint, discovered that much of the structure was unstable and that the tower and spire, pushed by the prevailing southwest sea breeze, was

Trinity Church.

tilting a foot to the north. The decision to repaint the outside off-white upset some but was in keeping with colonial practices, according to architectural historians. The happily restored church is open Monday to Saturday from 10 a.m. to 5 p.m. from June 15 to Labor Day, and afternoons in spring and fall. Sunday services are 8 a.m. and 10 a.m. in July and August, 8 and 11 the rest of the year. For information call 846-0660.

Hunter House, 54 Washington Street, on the Point. A National Historic Landmark, the Hunter House is considered by architectural historians to be one of the finest examples of a mid-eighteenth-century dwelling in existence. Aside from its pure lines and stately proportions, the house is rich in history. More accurately called the Nichols-Wanton-Hunter House, the house had its modest beginnings in 1748 when Jonathan Nichols bought the property on what was then called Water Street. Nichols was heavily engaged in the sea trade; he owned several ships and there was probably a wharf and warehouse buildings on the site. According to a city map of 1758, a one-chimney dwelling stood on the site.

Upon Nichols's death in 1757, the house was bought by Colonel Joseph Wanton Jr., a politically active merchant who added a south portion to the dwelling, giving it very much the appearance it has today. Both Wanton, a colonial deputy, and his father, governor of the colony, were staunch Tories and were forced into exile across the bay in 1775 as the rebellion heated up. With the arrival of British forces in 1776, Wanton came back to Newport, where he served as superintendent of police. But when the British withdrew three years later, the Wantons were forced to flee again. They died in exile, but Wanton Jr.'s Tory politics probably saved the house from destruction while an estimated 300 others on the Point and elsewhere in town were destroyed by the British.

When the French allies reached Newport in 1780, the house became headquarters for Admiral de Ternay, whose fleet delivered French commander Rochambeau and his troops to America. De Ternay's stay was brief; contracting a fever, he died on December 15, 1780 on his warship *Duc de Bourgogne,* anchored near the house. After several years of neglect, the house was purchased by William Hunter, a lawyer, U.S. senator, and ambassador, who landscaped the grounds and, mainly through his 44 years of ownership, gave his name to the house.

Today the house has been meticulously restored by the Preservation Society of Newport County. Although many of the original furnishings were lost, the house has been refurnished with authentic Queen Anne, Chippendale and Hepplewhite pieces made by the Townsend and Goddard families and other colonial craftsmen. The house is notable for its fine interior woodwork—six of the rooms contain floor-to-ceiling pine wainscoting "grained" to resemble finer hardwoods. The northeast parlor paneling is offset by marbleized Corinthian columns. The house and garden are open daily from late April through October from 10 a.m. to 5 p.m., weekends in spring and fall. Admission is $6 for adults, $3 for children.

Wanton-Lyman-Hazard House, at 17 Broadway, just up from Washington Square. Now situated somewhat incongruously in a commercial district, this restored house is one of the oldest in the city. Built between 1650 and 1700, its steeply pitched roof and central chimney are typical of the homes built by the early settlers. The interior walls are still covered with the original plaster made, in some cases, from ground shells and molasses. There's also a fine early colonial fireplace.

A number of notable residents lived at this address, including Martin Howard Jr., a Tory who had to flee for his life during the Stamp Act Riot of August 26, 1765. During the French occupation, the house was frequented by French officers courting Polly Lawton, a Quaker teenager considered one of the most charming young women on either side of the Atlantic. "A nymph rather than a woman . . . so much beauty, so much modesty," a count confided to his diary. Their attentions were to no avail—Polly married an American soldier, Major Daniel Lyman. A National Historic Landmark, the house has been furnished by the Newport Historical Society. There is a restored colonial garden out back. It is open to the public between June and Labor Day from 10 a.m. to 5 p.m. on Tuesday to Saturday. Admission is $3, free for children under 12. For information call the Historical Society at 846-0813.

Cliff Walk and Ocean Drive both offer unparalleled views of the Atlantic coastline. The Drive, which skirts the southern rim of Aquidneck, can be approached from two directions: from the east, it begins where Bellevue Avenue ends; from the west, you can pick it up at the end of Wellington Avenue, which runs along the south end of the harbor. At Brenton Point Park there is a large area for autos to turn off and park. You can stay in the car and watch the breakers, or venture across the street and pick out a bench. For a wider view, you can walk back through a ruined stable to the park's observation tower.

The strange collection of pillars rising from one section of the park is the Portuguese Navigators Monument, built in 1988 and not completely finished yet. The 16 pillars, of white sandstone quarried in Portugal, are an abstract representation of the compass rose (the navigator's compass), in particular one in the Portuguese city of Sagres, site of what is believed to have been the world's first navigational school. The sculpture is the work of architect and artist Joao Charters de Almeida.

Aside from the sea, numerous big houses, or mansions, will be seen on both sides of the Drive. Most are in private hands and not open to the public.

A few points of interest: Most of the large houses along Bellevue and Ocean Drive have their stories. One is Clarendon Court, on the east side of Bellevue a few houses beyond Marble House, opposite Rovensky Park. This is where Claus von Bulow either did (first trial) or did not (second trial) attempt to murder his wife, heiress Sunny von Bulow, with a lethal injection of insulin. The house was designed by Horace Trumbauer, architect of The Elms, in 1904, and is patterned after an eighteenth-century English house. The quiet park across the street was given to the city by John Rovensky, who owned Clarendon Court at one time.

The white mansion south of Clarendon Court is Miramar, another Trumbauer creation, from 1914, and was one of the last (and, some say, least successful) of the large classical summer palaces. It currently serves as corporate headquarters for a nursing home operation.

The last house on the left, before Bellevue makes a sharp right and becomes Ocean Avenue, is Rough Point, although you won't see it from the street because of the large gates blocking the view. The gates are testimony to the desire for privacy by the current owner, tobacco heiress Doris Duke, who founded the Newport Restoration Foundation responsible for rehabilitating many of Newport's finer colonial homes. The house, built in 1888–91 for Frederick Vanderbilt, can be viewed from the Cliff Walk on the water side.

Crossways, on Ocean Avenue, straight ahead after you make the turn past Bailey's Beach. Built by McKim, Mead and White, Crossways is notable for its four-column colonial portico. During the heyday of Newport society, it was more noted for being the summer residence of the imposing Mrs. Stuyvesant Fish, who reigned over Newport with the Vanderbilts and Astors. Mrs. Fish was a sort of Don Rickles of her set, abruptly cutting short her dinner parties and insulting her guests, who couldn't wait to be asked back for more abuse. "Make yourself at home," she told one group. "Certainly there is no one who wishes you were there more than I." Crossways, alas, now belongs to the condo set.

"Bubbling Rock" isn't a mansion, but rather a traffic stop that has become a minor attraction over the years with residents and visitors alike. Bubbling Rock is located about four-fifths of a mile north of Brenton Point Park, roughly opposite Price's Cove. It is found on the north side of Ocean Avenue. Look for a break in the vegetation and a gravel driveway leading to a locked gate (an entrance to Wrentham House). Set in the driveway is a mortar and rock mound about three feet high that was built in the 1940s as a traffic divider. The enterprising gardener who conceived it decided to embellish it a little to resemble a lighthouse. But passersby soon discovered that a handful of gravel dropped over the top would bounce off the embedded slates, creating the sound of falling water—hence the name. Broken slates have muted the tune somewhat, but it's still worth a try.

If you're in a walking mood, try the Cliff Walk, a narrow path that runs 3.45 miles between Easton's Beach (First Beach) and Bailey's Beach, or Spouting Rock Beach Club, the exclusive bathing club of the Newport elite whose membership, it's said, is inherited, not earned. Perhaps the best starting place is the eastern end of Narragansett Avenue, where you can scramble down Forty Steps for a closer look at the sea. From there heading south the walk twists, turns, and even tunnels between the ocean, many feet below, and the back lawns of some of the famous estates. The path brings you close to Marble House's Chinese teahouse. The walk was here long before the mansions were built, but some of the owners periodically have tried to block access to the public—one built two walls across the walk only to have them torn down by angry Newporters and tossed into the ocean below. The public and the state's concept of fishermen's rights of access to the shore have prevailed. The walk has been damaged by hurricanes and erosion over the years, but has been restored to mostly good condition by the Army Corps of Engineers. Just the same, there are several spots where the unwary stroller could take a precipitous fall to the rocks below.

Redwood Library, 50 Bellevue Avenue, at the corner of Redwood Street, was built in 1748. This National Historic Landmark was designed by Peter Harrison and is the oldest library building in America in continuous service. The building, which has been enlarged four times, is classical in style. Although built of wood, like most early buildings in Newport, the siding has been blasted to resemble stone. The library's lending service is private, but the building is open to the public. Writers Henry James and Edith Wharton stopped by and it's easy to see why; inside and out on the grounds, the library is one of the most pleasant and peaceful sites in the city. The Redwood has an excellent collection of Early American paintings and rare books. Open Monday through Saturday, 10 a.m. to 5 p.m. Admission is free.

3
MORE TO DO IN AND AROUND TOWN

THERE'S A LOT MORE TO NEWPORT than the mansions. In fact there's enough to keep you busy for a week or longer—museums, many more historical sites, and several organized tours on land or water. If you choose you can spend much of yoour time outdoors, visiting city parks and landmarks, attending one of many special events, going swimming, or learning to sail. Here are some of the options to help you plan your time.

MUSEUMS

Newport Historical Society, 82 Touro Street, just up from Washington Square. The Historical Society building incorporates the Sabbatarian Meeting House built in 1729. The Meeting

House is the oldest of its faith in the United States and contains a beautiful wineglass pulpit. The Society's collection contains rare and valuable paintings and fine period furniture, especially that made by the local Goddard and Townsend families.

The reference collection contains many manuscripts and historical documents that give the flavor and tempo of early colonial life in Newport, back when the city was an active center of trade, politics, and intrigue. Here's an example from a Newporter's letter of 1741, reprinted in the Boston Evening Post: "On Monday last our Governor and Council receiv'd advice from New-York that there were two Spanish privateers on the Coast, upon which it was ordered that the Colony Sloop should take a Cruise . . . and the next Day she sail'd with about an hundred stout men, commanded by Captain Benjamin Wickham, whose instructions are to go as far Westward as New York, and then to stretch to Eastward as far as Martha's Vineyard. It is said that one of the privateers is commanded by a French Man, whom in particular we are in great hopes Captain Wickham will meet with, that the Monsieur may be suitably corrected for dabbling in affairs that he has no Business with."

The first floor has changing exhibits. Unfortunately, what used to be a pleasant if cramped marine exhibit in the basement has been moved to the Museum of Yachting.

Upstairs, the library contains the second largest genealogical collection in Rhode Island and will do research for a small fee. The Society also conducts historical walking tours of Newport from June 15 through September on Friday and Saturday mornings at 10. Tours are $4 for adults, children under 12 free; admission to the Society building is free, but donations are welcome. For information call 846-0813.

International Tennis Hall of Fame in the Newport Casino, 194 Bellevue Avenue. Newport has good claim to calling itself the home of American tennis: One year after the Newport Casino was built in 1880, it became the site for the first National Men's Championship and all subsequent lawn tennis nationals

Court tennis in costume at Newport Casino (International Tennis Hall of Fame).

until 1915. National Grass Court championships are held here each year, as well as professional men's and women's tournaments.

Designed by Stanford White, the casino complex is a wonderful example of period architecture surrounding green grass courts that predate Wimbledon's. The stately atmosphere belies the fact that the casino was founded by two Newport society delinquents. Visiting British polo player Captain Henry Candy, acting on a dare from James Gordon Bennett, publisher and yachtsman, rode his horse onto the front porch of the ultra-staid Newport Reading Room club on Bellevue Avenue. The members were not amused; Candy was barred from the club and Bennett was reprimanded. Bennett's response was to build his own club, which soon became a gathering spot for Newport's best, especially during Tennis Week each August. The casino was designated a National Historic Landmark in 1987.

Today, the front portion of the complex houses the Hall of Fame and museum, billed as the largest tennis museum in the world. Housed on two floors, the museum contains at least a dozen rooms filled with every kind of tennis memorabilia, including equipment, trophies, period costumes, paintings and photographs. There is a Davis Cup Room and Davis Cup Theater where old tennis films are shown. The museum is open 10 a.m. to 5 p.m. from May to September, 11 a.m. to 4 p.m. the rest of the year. Admission is $4 for adults, $2.50 for children. For information or event tickets call 849-3990.

The Newport Art Museum, 76 Bellevue Avenue. Designed by Richard Morris Hunt, the J.N.A. Griswold house that now serves as the art museum's main building is a prime example of mid-Victorian "stick style" architecture in which vertical and diagonal "sticks" on the exterior suggest the underlying structure. The museum has regular exhibits by internationally known artists in half a dozen galleries, including the adjacent mausoleum-like Cushing Gallery. There's also a permanent collection of nineteenth- and twentieth-century American artwork. Open Tuesday to Saturday from 10 a.m. to 5 p.m., Sunday 1–5 p.m. Admission is $2 for adults, $1 for senior citizens; children under 18 free. For information call 847-0179.

Newport Artillery Company, 23 Clarke Street, just off Washington Square. Chartered in 1741 by King George, the company is the oldest militia in continuous service in America. The headquarters, built in 1836 in solid Greek Revival style, houses military uniforms and weapons from colonial times to the present, as well as artifacts from more than 100 countries. Open June 1 to September 30 from 10 a.m. to 4 p.m., Sunday from 12–4 p.m. Admission is $3 adults, $1.50 children.

More to Do   51

Samuel Whitehorne House, 416 Thames Street. Operated by Doris Duke's Newport Restoration Foundation, the Whitehorne House was built in 1811 and is a fine example of Federal period architecture when brick was being introduced in the construction of residences. Captain Samuel White-horne, Jr., a prosperous merchant, was the original owner, but shipping losses bankrupted him and he lost the house at auction in 1844.

Beautifully restored, the house contains many fine period furniture pieces, including works by Goddard and Town-send, and silver and pewter made by Newport silversmiths between 1740 and 1840. Outside, there's a garden typical of the Federal period with early varieties of plants rarely seen now. Open Saturdays, Sundays, Mondays, and holidays from 10 a.m. to 4 p.m. Admission is $3.50 for adults, $1 for students. Open by appointment other days. Call 847-2448.

Hammersmith Farm, off Harrison Avenue as you begin Ocean Drive from the west. The main house at Hammersmith Farm, where Jacqueline Bouvier grew up and she and her husband President John Kennedy summered, has been converted into a museum with all original furnishings. Jacqueline's

Hammersmith Farm, once the Kennedy summer White House.

childhood bedroom is on display, as well as the room where President Kennedy signed bills while using Hammersmith as a kind of summer White House. The formal gardens outside, including a playhouse garden, are open. Not all of the farm is public—the Hugh D. Auchincloss family retains ownership of the windmill-like guest house and the venerable "house of four chimneys." Open 10 a.m. to 7 p.m. daily from Memorial Day through Labor Day weekend. Admission is $5 for adults, $2 for children ages 6–12. Call 846-0420.

Museum of Yachting at Fort Adams State Park, off Ocean Drive. Housed in a nineteenth-century brick building on the waterfront, the Museum of Yachting offers a tour of the history of yachting through its displays of photos, painting, boating gear, and various kinds of vessels. The America's Cup Gallery traces the history of this prestigious event which took place off Newport from the glorious J-boat days of the 1930s when Harold S. Vanderbilt manned the helm, to the era of the 12-meters when the Cup was lost to Australia in 1983. There is also a Singlehanded Hall of Fame that honors intrepid sailors from around the world who have taken to sea alone, many of whom have Newport ties. Outside, you may see the museum's own J-class sloop, *Shamrock V*, or its sister ship *Endeavour*. The museum is open daily from May 15 to November 1 from 10 a.m. to 5 p.m. Admission is $2 for adults and $1 for seniors, with children under 12 free. For information call 847-1018. Instead of driving to the museum, you can take a launch (about $5, tour included) from Bowen's Wharf. Tickets and information are available at the nautical-looking shed on Bowen's, which is actually the deckhouse from the *Shamrock V*.

Looming beside the museum is Fort Adams, a sturdy granite structure that is one of the largest seacoast fortifications built in the United States. During the Revolution patriots began fortifying this strategic point overlooking the entrance to Narragansett Bay, but the occupying British destroyed their work. In 1799, the fort was rededicated and named for President John Adams.

It fell into disrepair until the War of 1812 put a scare into Congress and work began in earnest to build a fort that could withstand attack from land or sea. Begun in 1824, the fort took 33 years to complete and, in fact, was never attacked. It served briefly as the U.S. Naval Academy in the early years of the Civil War when Annapolis was threatened. Unfortunately, public tours of the fort have been suspended because of unsafe conditions inside. The surrounding park, however, which offers a superb spot to fish, swim, or watch yachts come and go, is open daily from 6 a.m. to 11 p.m. Rangers collect a nominal fee for each passenger car from Memorial Day to Labor Day. Admission is free the rest of the year.

Naval War College Museum, Coasters Harbor Island, through Gate 1 at the southern end of the Naval Education and Training Center. The War College is where Navy officers get their advanced training. The museum, located in Founders Hall, offers exhibits on the history of the "art and science" of naval warfare, as well as local seafaring history. Open Monday to Friday, 10 a.m. to 4 p.m., and weekends 12-4 p.m. from June to September. Admission is free. For information call 841-4052.

CHURCHES

St. Mary's Church, corner of Spring Street and Memorial Boulevard. Built between 1848–52, this English Gothic Church was designed by Patrick Keeley of New York. It is the seat of the oldest Catholic parish in the state; Jacqueline Bouvier and Senator John F. Kennedy, later thirty-fourth president, were married here on September 12, 1953. St. Mary's was designated a National Shrine in 1968. Open Monday through Friday from 7–11 a.m., except holidays.

Channing Memorial Church, on Pelham Street across from Touro Park, is dedicated to William Ellery Channing, a Newporter credited with founding the Unitarian Church in America. Channing (his statue stands across the street in the park) was a philosopher, writer and friend to many Newport literary figures. He did most of his preaching at the Union Church in Portsmouth and in the Boston area, but summered in Newport. The existing church, which was built in the mid-nineteenth century, contains two beautiful stained glass windows by John La Farge, Julia Ward Howe's pew, and a bronze plaque by Augustus Saint-Gaudens. Open by appointment (846-0643).

United Baptist Church, 30 Spring Street, behind the Colony House. Dr. John Clarke was the founder and first pastor (1638) of this church. In 1663, Clarke obtained a royal charter for Rhode Island from King Charles II, which set a precedent for the colonies by guaranteeing full freedom of religious pursuits. The church contains a room displaying items of historical interest. Open daily from 9 a.m. to 4 p.m. (847-3210).

Newport Congregational Church, corner Spring and Pelham streets. Called Church of the Patriots because its members refused to side with Mother England during the Revolution and saw their original church building on Mill Street converted to a barracks for British troops and later a hospital for French forces. The church was heavily damaged; all that exists today is the cornerstone, bearing the legend, "For Christ and Peace," now at the parish house. The existing church was built in 1857 and contains an interior designed by artist John La Farge and well worth seeing. The walls have a distinct Byzantine flavor and the opalescent stained glass windows were made from a technique devised by La Farge. Open Tuesdays and Thursdays from 10 a.m. to noon from Memorial Day to Labor Day, or by appointment. Call 849-2238.

Quaker Meeting House, corner of Marlborough and Farewell streets, one block north of Washington Square. Recently restored, the Friends Great Meeting House was built in 1699 and is the oldest in the country. An outstanding example of seventeenth-century architecture, the meeting house contains models and architectural exhibits, as well as changing exhibits on Quaker life and dress. The Quakers, persecuted in Massachusetts, found a welcome home in Newport. There they rose to political and commercial power, building many of the fine captain's homes in the neighboring Point Section. (The Friends, however, did incur resentment on occasion, especially during the Revolution, for what was considered to be an overly pacifistic attitude toward the British. In several instances, windows in Quaker homes were broken by angry "patriots.") Open mid-June to September, from 10 a.m. to 5 p.m. Call Newport Historical Society (846-0813) for an appointment. Tour costs $2 for adults, children under 12 free.

STATUES

The Wave, at Newport Bay Club, corner of Thames Street and America's Cup Avenue. The most public of public statues in the city, *The Wave,* sculpted by Jamestowner Kay Worden, depicts a pair of feet disappearing into a bronze breaking wave. Since the statue appeared in 1983, passersby have regularly stuck on bandage strips or a pair of socks. Worden says she once saw an enterprising teenager charging tourists 15 cents for a chance to rub the feet for good luck. "People participate in it a lot. I think it's neat," Worden says of her original work. Another of her sculptures, *The Hurdy Gurdy,* can be seen in the courtyard at Brick Market Place, several blocks to the north. Worden can be reached at her studio at 423-1758.

Perry Monument, Touro Park, facing Bellevue Avenue. Matthew Perry, a commodore in the U.S. Navy, negotiated the opening of Japan to trade with the West in 1853. This memorial, executed by John Quincy Adams Ward, is appropriately Oriental in character. Look closely at the frieze that runs around the statue. The dedication of this monument to one of Newport's favorite sons on October 3, 1868, was the occasion of a great celebration. There is a similar monument in Perrotti Park, off America's Cup Avenue.

William Ellery Channing, also in Touro Park, facing Channing Memorial Park. Channing, a noted Unitarian minister and grandson of William Ellery, a Newporter who signed the Declaration of Independence, was a philosopher who even pondered the beneficial effects of Newport's notorious fogs, which, he said, "are proverbially a good cosmetic, and there is a tradition that the fair daughters of Newport owed their lustrous complexions to sleeping with their heads out the window when the mists of the sea prevailed." The statue is the work of William Clark Noble.

George Washington, in front of the Redwood Library, Bellevue Avenue. This is one of seven copies in bronze of a statue by the French sculptor Jean-Antoine Houdon. The original is located in Virginia.

Statue of George Washington at the Redwood Library.

Rochambeau, King Park on Wellington Avenue. The street may be named for the famed British naval hero, but Newport chose to remember the Compte de Rochambeau with a statue at the spot where the French general landed with 5,000 troops to help the rebel cause.

Organized Tours

Some visitors will want to do at least some of their touring on an organized basis. It's a good way to get a quick feel for the layout—and some of the history—of Newport.

Viking Tours (847-6921) offers three basic tours. The first, a narrated tour of the city ($11 adults, $7.50 children) lasts about two hours and includes more than 20 miles of Newport scenery, including the colonial sections, Ocean Drive, and the mansions. On this tour, you don't actually get off the bus. The second tour ($17 adults, $10.50 children) includes narration plus a stop at Marble House for the Preservation Society tour. The third tour ($22 adults, $13 children) combines the narration with a visit to The Breakers. The tours are run daily from April 1 to the end of October, and on Saturdays year-round. Tickets can be purchased at the Gateway Center.

Viking is one of several firms offering harbor tours. The first ($6 adults, $5 for "juniors" 12–16, $4 for children 4–11) is a one-hour narrated cruise through the harbor and East Passage. It's a great way to get a fresh view of the city and a nice excursion on a summer afternoon or evening. The second tour ($11 adults, $4.50 children) lasts about two and one-half hours, including a stop and guided tour at Hammersmith Farm. The boats depart from Goat Island, just south of the island causeway.

Oldport Marine (849-2111) on Sayer's Wharf, downtown, offers a one-hour narrated tour of the harbor aboard *Amazing Grace*. The fare is $6 for adults, $4 for children. The harbor tours offered by both of these firms are an exceptional value in an often pricey town.

Sightsailing of Newport (849-3333) provides sailboat tours of Newport Harbor and Narragansett Bay, following a route similar to the motorized vessels. Tours depart Bowen's Wharf (wind permitting) at two-hour intervals from 10 a.m. to 6 p.m. from Memorial Day to Columbus Day. Six passengers a trip, and you may take the helm if you wish. $20 per person.

Newport Harbor Tours (683-2738) on Goat Island. Two-hour tours on 23-foot sloops. Call for reservations, but buy tickets at Gateway Center. $20 per person.

Old Colony & Newport Railway (849-8048) offers a great one-and-one-half hour rail trip along the shore to Portsmouth, where the train makes a stop at Green Animals topiary garden. If you decide to tour the gardens, admission is $6 for adults, $3 for children 6–11. The railroad operates Sunday and holidays in spring and fall, and Saturdays, Sundays, and holidays from July 1 to September 2. Cost is $6 for adults, $5 for seniors, $4 for children, and $15 for a family. Tickets available at Gateway Center or the tiny railroad station just north of the information center on America's Cup Avenue.

There are also several air tours of Newport that originate from Newport State Airport, Forest Avenue, Middletown, accessible from West or East Main Road.

Corporate Air Newport (848-5550) offers a 20-minute ride over the city, along the coast, and over the mansions. $40 for two passengers; $60 for three or more.

Newport Helicoptors Inc. (846-8877) gives 20-minute aerial tours for $50 per person, with a two-person minimum.

AREA ATTRACTIONS

Whitehall, on Berkeley Avenue in Middletown off Green End Avenue, is a fine colonial farmhouse built in 1729 by British philosopher and cleric, Dean George Berkeley (pronounced Bark-ley). Berkeley, later to become bishop of Cloyne, Ireland, arrived in Newport that year accompanied by his bride and a scheme to open up commerce and bring religion to the "savages" of Bermuda. "The town of Newport," he wrote home, "contains six thousand souls, and is the most thriving place in all America for bigness." While waiting for the king to grant him £20,000 for his mission, Berkeley preached at Trinity Church, helped found the Redwood Library, and made Whitehall a center for religious and philosophical discussion. The dean gave up after three years and returned to Ireland; his house was taken over by a succession of tavern keepers, served as quarters for British troops during the Revolution, and eventually fell into disrepair. Now owned by the Rhode Island chapter of the National Society of Colonial Dames of America, the house has been restored and is open to the public daily from July 1 to Labor Day from 10 a.m. to 5 p.m., or by appointment. Admission is $3 for adults, $1 for children 6–16. For information call 846-3790 or 846-3116.

Whitehall, Dean Berkeley's home.

Norman Bird Sanctuary, Third Beach Road, Middletown, is a 450-acre bird and wildlife sanctuary with miles of nature trails open to the public. There are a few local species in captivity (while on the mend), but everything else you're lucky enough to see will be in the wild. There are guided tours by appointment for groups of 10 or more and regular Sunday morning birdwalks. One of the big attractions here is Hanging Rock, a striking mass of rock fifty feet high that overlooks the Atlantic. Dean Berkeley is said to have written part of his anti-freethinkers treatise *Alciphron* here, in a recessed haven now called "Bishop Berkeley's Chair." Open daily 9 a.m. to 5 p.m. (no dogs, please). Admission is $2, children accompanied by an adult free. For information about tours or special events call 846-2577.

Purgatory Chasm, Purgatory Road, Middletown, on the cliff overlooking Second Beach. The chasm is a narrow but deep cleft in the rocky cliff caused by thousands of years of erosion by the sea below. Or was it? Indian legend says it came about when the Devil repeatedly chopped away at the head of an uncooperative Indian maiden. There are countless other stories about lovers who dared each other to hop across the fissure. Don't try it—it's more than 160 feet straight down.

Prescott Farm, West Main Road (RI 114) in Middletown. Shortly before midnight on July 9, 1777, a band of 40 raiding colonists, led by Colonel William Barton, landed their rowboats on the west shore of British-controlled Aquidneck Island. Splitting into five groups, they sneaked up to a farmhouse owned by Mrs. John Overing, captured the guard, and burst inside. When they left minutes later, they took with them (still in his nightclothes) General William Prescott, commander of the British occupying troops and the highest-ranking prisoner taken during the Revolution. Prescott was later exchanged for a captured American general. Barton was awarded a sword by Congress, and the house in Middletown has been known as Prescott Farm ever since. In addition to the house itself, the

Prescott Farm, Portsmouth.

farm complex owned by Doris Duke's Restoration Foundation includes a late eighteenth-century grain mill moved to the site several years ago. There's also a guardhouse and a country store that offers cornmeal ground at the mill. On calm days visitors can tour the carefully restored mill, and on breezy days you can stand at a safe distance and watch the sails go around. Open daily April to December from 10 a.m. to 4 p.m. Admission is $1.50 for adults, 75 cents for children. For group rates or other information call 847-6230 or 849-7300.

Green Animals topiary in Portsmouth.

Green Animals is a splendid topiary garden managed by the Preservation Society on Cory Lane in Portsmouth, off RI 114. The gardens, started by Thomas Brayton about 1880, contain some 80 sculptured trees and shrubs, formal flower beds, and fruit and vegetable patches. The animal figures—carved from California privet—are the best part. There's a camel, a giraffe, a bear, and many others to pick out as you wander down intricate pathways. A garden shop sells various herbs, plants, and flowers. The adjacent Brayton House overlooking Narragansett Bay contains a child's Victorian toy museum. Admission is $5 for adults, $3 for children 6–11, and is well worth it. Call 847-1000 for information.

Portsmouth Abbey Chapel, Cory Lane, Portsmouth. The Chapel of St. Gregory at this Benedictine abbey and prep school is beautifully contemporary. Designed by Pietro Belluschi, it contains a wire sculpture by Richard Lippold. The chapel is open to the public daily from 8 a.m. to 4:30 p.m.

Hessian Hole, Cory Lane, on the grounds of Portsmouth Abbey. After the Battle of Rhode Island, according to legend, 30 dead Hessian soldiers (Germans fighting as mercenaries for the British) were buried in a pit just west of where the Abbey now stands. Nearby flows Bloody Run Brook, so named because it supposedly ran red for days after the burial. There's some doubt about where the actual burial site is, but you may want to follow the brook and look for a noticeable depression in the land.

Black Regiment Memorial, in Portsmouth at the junction of RI 114 and RI 24. During the Battle of Rhode Island, in which Continental troops were attempting to retreat after an unsuccessful siege of Newport, the Americans had to hold off several attacks by the British while awaiting boats to remove them from Aquidneck. It was here on August 29, 1778, that the First Rhode Island Regiment, composed entirely of slaves earning their freedom through military service, whipped the Hessian allies of the British. Lafayette later called the battle "the best fought action of the war" and wept because he had missed most of it. The retreating regiment inflicted heavy casualties on the enemy in rear-guard fighting without losing a single soldier. A flagpole and a stone monument now mark the spot where America's first black troops earned their glory.

BEACHES

Newport and its neighboring towns have been blessed with a plentiful supply of good bathing beaches. And because the Gulf Stream lies relatively close offshore, the waters are warm by New England standards—certainly warmer than on much of Cape Cod, for example. Although some of the better spots along the southern tip of the island have been staked out by private clubs, most of the sandy stretches remain in the public domain. On the hottest summer days, especially on weekends, parking can be a problem. To be assured of a spot, arrive well before noon or wait until 4 or 5 p.m. when the crowds have gone and the water and air are still warm from the day's sun.

Easton's Beach, also known as First Beach and Newport Beach, is a three-quarter-mile stretch from the northern edge of the Cliff Walk in Newport to the Middletown line. Access is easy—just follow Memorial Boulevard down the hill to the entrance. During Victorian times, the water at Easton's was considered an elixir and the infirm were carted down for a dip. Bathing was a much more modest activity at that time; the sexes were strictly segregated, women getting the first turn at 10 a.m. "At noon all this changed," recalled George C. Mason in his chronicle, *Newport and Its Cottages.* "The white flag is hauled down; a red bunting takes its place; the ladies retire, and for a few hours the beach is given up exclusively to gentlemen." Newport's largest public beach has three parking lots accommodating something under 700 cars. Cost for nonresidents is $5 per car weekdays, $10 on weekends. There's limited on-street parking, but don't park in a restricted zone—you'll be tagged or towed. Bathhouses are available for $5 a day, and there's a concession stand selling the usual beach fare. On weekends and many evenings, a carousel and bumper boat operation is open. Surfing is permitted in a restricted area at the east end of the beach. The beach is open from Memorial Day weekend to Labor Day. Lifeguards are on duty from 9 a.m. to 6 p.m.

Sachuest Beach (Second Beach) in Middletown is the most popular beach in the area, with a long expanse of dunes and sand running between Hanging Rock and a former U.S. Navy radio site on Sachuest Point. To get there, follow Memorial Boulevard or Aquidneck Avenue to Purgatory Road. Public parking on pavement can handle up to 1,000 cars. Parking for nonresidents is $10 weekdays, $15 weekends and holidays.

Third Beach off Third Beach Road in Middletown. Smaller but less crowded than its cousin up the road, Third Beach is ideal for younger swimmers, with little or no surf and warmer waters from the mouth of the Sakonnet River. Parking is $10 weekdays, $15 weekends and holidays.

King Park on Wellington Avenue in Newport is the people's beach. It's close to town, looking north across the harbor, and parking along Wellington is free. Lifeguards are on duty from 9 a.m. to 6 p.m. from Memorial Day to Labor Day, and on most hot days the beach will be crowded with families. Charcoal grills and picnic tables are available, and you can sit on the grass under the trees or down on the sand. The shallow portion of the water is marked off with buoys for kids, and there's a raft with slide for the more daring swimmers. On land, there are free bathhouses and swings and slides.

Fort Adams State Park, off Harrison Avenue on the way to Ocean Drive. This modest beach on the south side of Brenton Cove is the perfect place for family swimming. There's a roped-off area for budding swimmers and plenty of picnic tables and charcoal grills. Lifeguards are on duty from 10 a.m. to 6 p.m. between Memorial Day and Labor Day. Entrance fee is $2 for out-of-state vehicles other than bicycles.

Gooseberry Beach, off Ocean Avenue, shares a cove with private Hazard's Beach on the west and is one cove over from exclusive Bailey's Beach to the east. As well as an attractive setting, Gooseberry offers safe ocean bathing for families. The parking lot has room for 150 cars, but there is a modest fee. Restrooms and a concession stand are available.

Bailey's Beach (East), or "Reject Beach," as it's sometimes called, is at the junction of Bellevue and Ocean Avenues. Unless you're on good terms with one of today's Four Hundred, this is as close as you'll get to the most exclusive bathing in Newport. You will also have to come by foot or by bike, since there's no parking area. But that's all right. The swimming itself is excellent and there's often good surf. And you won't be subject to the turn-of-the-century restrictions even Vanderbilts were compelled to observe. According to Consuelo, Alva's much put-upon daughter, the women of Bailey's, even away from the prying public eyes of Easton's Beach, followed a strict dress code as they suited up for swimming: "My skirt almost touched the ground. It was considered immodest to wear them shorter. My dresses had high, tight, whalebone collars. A corset laced my waist to the eighteen inches fashion decreed."

Sandy Point Beach in Portsmouth is about 20 minutes from town at the foot of Sandy Point Avenue, off RI 138. It's a pleasant family beach with no surf and warm Sakonnet River water. Sandy Point opens Memorial Day weekend and closes Labor Day, with lifeguards on duty from 9 a.m. to 6 p.m. There are restrooms with an outside shower, picnic benches and charcoal grills. No concession stand, but a snack truck stops by regularly.

Special Events

One of the things that distinguishes Newport from other small resorts is a busy schedule of summer events. Even residents must budget time and money during the busiest months of July and August, forgoing one event to see another. Here are some of the best.

Secret Gardens Tour offers visitors a chance to peer behind the garden walls of a variety of private gardens in the colonial Point area. With as many as 20 gardens included, the tour can easily consume much of an afternoon. Generally takes place the third weekend in June (when the hollyhocks are in bloom). Tickets are $10, with the proceeds going to the Benefactors of the Arts. For information call the Gateway Center at 1-800-326-6030, or 401-849-8098.

Newport Music Festival—Brahms at The Breakers, Mozart at Marble House—the Music Festival each year brings classical music to the mansions and other beautiful settings around town, outdoors and in. The programming (three concerts a day) and level of musicianship is on a par with the Spoleto Festival in Charleston, South Carolina, minus the dance and opera. Usually scheduled the second and third weeks of July. For information call 401-846-1133. Tickets available at the Gateway Center or via the box office (849-0700).

Newport Jazz and Folk Festivals—George Wein's Jazz Festival, begun in the 1950s, helped put Newport on the contemporary map. The Folk Festival, added in the sixties, drew many more thousands to the city to hear Pete Seeger, Bob Dylan, and "discoveries" such as Joan Baez. Huge crowds and raucous behavior killed the outdoor fests for a while, but Wein has returned with smaller programs in the more sedate setting of Fort Adams. Both festivals offer a blend of old favorites and new talent, and the music, as always, is great. The Folk Festival generally happens the first or second week of August, the Jazz the following week. For information and tickets call the box office at 847-3709 or 847-3710, or contact the Gateway Center at 849-8098. Box office address is 270 Thames Street, Newport, RI 02840.

Black Ships Festival—An international festival commemorating the relationship between the United States and Japan that began when Commodore Matthew Perry, at the request of President Millard Fillmore, pressured the Japanese to open their ports to foreign ships in 1853. Sponsored by the Japan-America Society, the week-long schedule of events, usually the last week in July, includes cultural programs like origami (art of folding paper) and flower arranging, and some events that are as much fun as cultural, such as a sumo wrestling competition. Incidentally, there are no "black ships"—that's how the Japanese characterized Perry's fleet as it lay at anchor off their shores. Call 846-2720 for information.

PGA Seniors Golf—The old pros' circuit visits Newport each summer at the Newport Country Club, on Harrison Avenue near Ocean Drive. The private club opened in 1893 and was the site of the first American amateur golf championship. Information about tickets and dates (usually the second weekend in July) can be obtained by calling the club (846-9227) or the local tournament office (847-9810).

Pro Tennis—The Newport Casino/Tennis Hall of Fame hosts professional men's and women's tennis each summer. The setting is intimate, the atmosphere incomparable.

The Miller Lite Hall of Fame men's tournament is usually the second week of July, two weeks after Wimbledon. These aren't the biggest stars, but still some of the best as well as those on the verge of top rankings. In the early 1970s, for example, the young John McEnroe played and blustered: After an objectionable call, he warned one umpire not to "walk the streets of Newport tonight." McEnroe returned to the Casino in 1991 to participate in Davis Cup play.

The Virginia Slims tour, always with a few of the top stars, generally takes place a week or so after the men's. This event usually outdraws the men's tennis, so reserve ahead. For information call the Casino at 846-4567.

Virginia Slims tennis action at the Newport Casino/Tennis Hall of Fame.

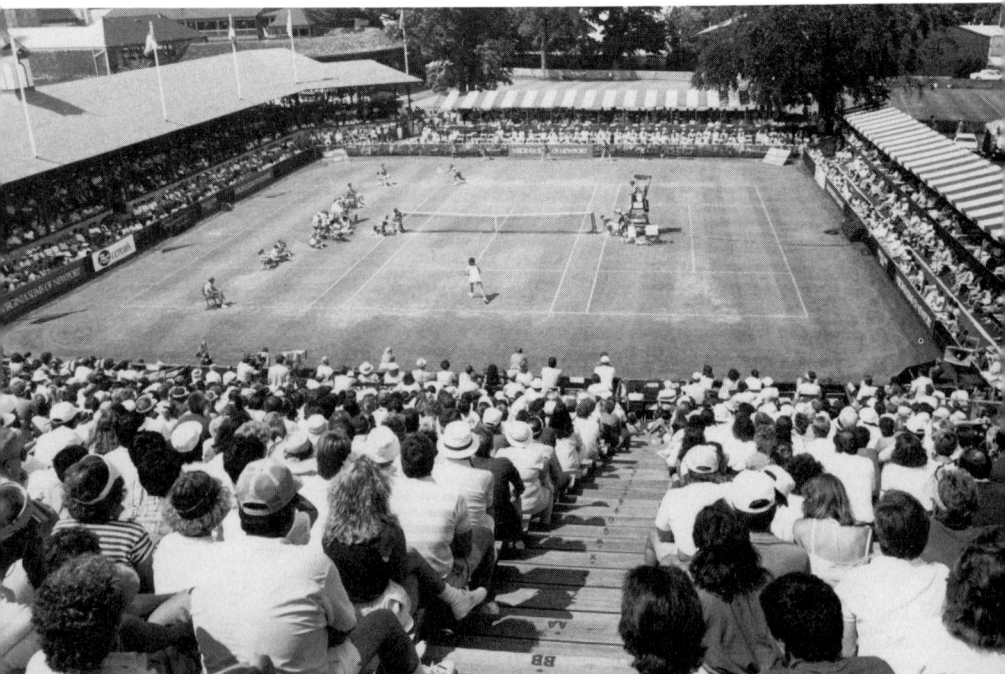

Classic Yacht Regatta—One of the last of the season's regattas, the Classic Yacht Regatta on Labor Day weekend is one event easy for spectators to enjoy. Some of the most beautiful wooden yachts in America take part in several days of racing and parading through the harbor. You can go out on a spectator boat or enjoy the show for free from several vantage points around the harbor. For information call the Museum of Yachting at 847-1018.

Boat Shows—There are several major boat shows in Newport each summer, including the Small Boat Show in the spring, the Newport International Sailboat Show the first week of September, and the International Powerboat Show shortly after. Call the Newport Yachting Center (846-1600) for information.

SPORTS

Perhaps because of the natural attractions of sea and shore, Newport has relatively limited facilities for sports like golf or tennis. Here's a list of those open to the public.

Tennis

Newport Casino, Bellevue Avenue. (846-4567). The same grass courts that Ashe, Evert, McEnroe and Navratilova have played on are open to the public, from May 25 to October 15, except during tournaments. Fee is $35 per person for an hour and a half of court time.

City of Newport Courts at five locations in the city. Courts are free.

>POP FLACK, behind the Almac's shopping center on Bellevue. Four courts. Lights.
>
>HUNTER, off Third Street, in the north end of the city. Two courts.
>
>VERNON, on Caswell Avenue off Vernon Avenue in the north end, near the Middletown line. Four courts.

MURPHY, in the south end, has courts at Murphy Field on Carroll Avenue.

ROGERS HIGH SCHOOL, nearby on Old Fort Road, has six courts.

Tennis Indoor Club, Memorial Boulevard, one block down from Bellevue (849-4777). The fee for these indoor courts is $25 per hour.

Squash

Newport Squash Racquets, 8 Freebody Street (846-1011). Three singles courts just off Memorial Boulevard, one block from Bellevue Avenue. Fee is $8 per person for 45 minutes, racquet and ball included.

Golf

Green Valley Country Club, 371 Union Street, between RI 138 and RI 114 (683-2162). Eighteen holes, public driving range. Fees are $20 daily.

Jamestown Country Club, 245 Conanicus Avenue, Jamestown (423-9930). This is a town-owned course; take the first (Jamestown) exit immediately after crossing Newport Bridge and head toward the center of town. Nine holes. Fees are $8 weekdays, $9 weekends for nine holes; $12 weekdays, $13 weekends if you play 18 holes.

Mountaup Country Club, Anthony Road, Portsmouth, just north of Ramada Inn and adjacent to Sakonnet River Bridge on RI 24 (683-9107). Eighteen holes. Daily fees are $27 for 18 holes, $14 if you play just nine.

Pocasset Country Club, 807 Bristol Ferry Road (683-2266). Follow RI 114 (West Main Road) through Portsmouth. At Mount Hope Bridge, go straight. Club is at land's end. Nine holes. Fee is $10 for nine holes, $12 if you go around twice.

Sailing

Sail Newport, Fort Adams State Park (849-8385). Nonprofit group that offers sailing instruction as well as half-day and day charters. Those renting boats, of course, are asked to demonstrate competency. Sail Newport has several types of small boats for rent, including J-22s. Fees on weekdays are $75 for three hours, $225 for the day; on weekends, $95 and $285. Smaller 18-footers (Fox or Tempest) available for $40 for three hours, $120 the day, weekdays; $45 and $135 weekends. If you plan to be around for some time or to make several trips within the year, it might make sense to join Sail Newport ($75 adults, $25 youth) and save substantially on rentals.

Newport Sailing School (683-2738 or 1-256-1595) offers 9- and 13-hour learn-to-sail programs on 23-foot sloops. One hour of classroom preparation. The short course, which is spread over two days, is $240 per person; the 13-hour, three-day course is $290.

Windsurfing

J-Class Boats (849-3060). If you have something larger in mind, you can rent either *Shamrock V* or *Endeavour*, the two restored J-class boats. For $6,000 a day plus expenses ($25,000 the week), you can take up to 19 friends along on the 120-foot *Shamrock V*, built in 1930 as an America's Cup challenger by Sir Thomas Lipton. Sister ship *Endeavour*, a 1934 Cup contender, is available for charter at $15,000 a day, $60,000 a week.

Island Windsurfing, 86 Aquidneck Avenue, Middletown (846-4421). Located near the beaches, just down the hill from Newport, Island Windsurfing rents rigs ($35 a day, $50 a day for advanced boards) and also offers two levels of lessons. A two-hour introductory session is $30; the advanced course, six hours over two days, costs $90. Lessons given either at Third Beach in Middletown or at Fort Adams State Park in Newport.

Fishing

There's some good surf fishing in the Newport area. Bass, bluefish, and blackfish all run fairly steadily from spring to late fall. Best places to fish are along Ocean Drive—at Agassiz Beach near Castle Hill, off the rocks at Brenton Point, or at state-run King's Beach near Price's Cove. Beavertail on the southern tip of Jamestown is also good. Good sources of information are Edwards Fishing Tackle, 36 Aquidneck Avenue, Middletown (846-4521) or, in Jamestown, Gregory Zeek of Zeek's Creek Bait & Tackle, 194 North Road (423-1170). If you're in town on a Friday, check Steven Baines' weekly fishing report in the *Newport Daily News,* the city's daily newspaper.

Charter fishing is surprisingly scarce in Newport given its ocean location, but there are several boats offering offshore and inshore trips. There also are a number of boats operating from Point Judith in Narragansett, a 35-minute drive from Newport. For information about area fishing charters, write the R.I. Party & Charter Boat Association, P.O. Box 3198, Narragansett, RI, 02882. On Aquidneck, the *Mayflower* (846-7225) makes six-hour trips for one, two, or three passengers. Cost for adults is $55/person for sport fishing, $35/person for bottom fishing (tautog, scup, flounder); $45 and $30 for each child under 12. FISHIN' OFF (849-9642) provides full or half-day charters aboard a 36-foot Trojan. The boat accommodates six passengers. Charter fee is $350 for a half day, $600 all day; offshore tuna fishing costs $700 for the day.

Spectator Sports

Sunset League Baseball, at Cardines Field, corner of America's Cup Avenue and Marlborough Street, across from the Gateway Center. For just $1 for adults, 50 cents for kids, you can take in a Sunset League baseball game. The league, started in 1919, is reputed to be the oldest surviving amateur circuit and features college talent, sometimes pros, and prospects. Cardines

Field, around since 1908, is older even than Boston's Fenway Park. Where else can you watch a baseball game with colonial houses crowding the outfield fence? Games begin at 7 p.m. weekdays, 1 or 3 p.m. on Saturdays.

Newport Jai Alai (or Hi Li, as their sign advertises) (849-5000), Admiral Kalbfus Road. The only fronton in the area (there are two in Connecticut) is just off the second exit ramp from the Newport Bridge. Pari-mutuel betting, but the rapid-paced Basque game is worth watching even if you don't gamble. Games nightly except Sunday at 7 p.m., noon matinees several times a week. General admission is $2; reserved seats cost several dollars more. There's a restaurant on the premises, the Sala del Toro, where you can watch the games on closed circuit television. Dates change, but the season generally runs from May through October.

4
THREE WALKING TOURS

 ⚜⚜⚜⚜

ONE OF NEWPORT'S UNIQUE FEATURES is the sense of living history you get as you walk the streets. Newport has more than four hundred colonial houses—more than any city in the country—most of which are not museums, but still functioning as houses. On a given street you may find homes reflecting a variety of architectural trends spanning almost three hundred years. A few are in disrepair, some have been altered beyond recognition, but many have been restored to their original condition.

Ironically, it was Newport's decline as a commercial power after the trials of the Revolution that contributed to the saving of many of its colonial buildings. After three years of British occupation and several more on a war footing, Newport was poor and depleted of resources and people. Those houses that survived destruction during the war were kept in their existing condition. Newporters were lucky to have roofs over their heads and did not renovate or tear down the old houses to be rebuilt in a new style. Most of the seventeenth-century medieval-style houses are gone, but the city has kept its core of eighteenth- and nineteenth-century dwellings. Starting in the 1940s when the Preservation Society of Newport County was created to preserve the Hunter House, a number of organizations were formed to save the city's architectural heritage. Tobacco heiress Doris Duke underwrote the Newport Restoration Foundation, which since 1968 has been responsible for restoring many colonial homes in Newport. Other groups included Operation Clapboard and the Oldport Association. More than a few dwellings also have been preserved and restored by private individuals. The process goes on.

Most of the city's colonial homes are within easy walking distance of each other. Take your time, block out the hum of traffic, pause to look over a picket fence at a garden, and you just may find yourself transported a century or two back in time.

1. WASHINGTON SQUARE AND HISTORIC HILL

Time: under an hour. Parking: three lots are convenient to various points of the tour—the municipal lot on Touro Street in Washington Square, the municipal lot on Mary Street off Thames, and the Long Wharf Mall's north lot, which charges a fee in summer. If you can find a space on the street, take it. You'll easily be back within the required two-hour limit.

Begin at Washington Square. The square, with its central parade, was the commercial, political and social center of colonial Newport. Here Newporters gathered to trade goods and swap gossip; here offenders were whipped or put in stocks; here proclamations that changed the course of the colony's— and the country's—future were read; here the colonial troops drilled, and here the early demonstrations against the British that led to war were staged.

BRICK MARKET, 127 Thames Street at the foot of the square, was the focus of commerce for the city. Commissioned by the Long Wharf merchants as a market and warehouse, this handsome building was designed by Peter Harrison and completed in 1762. A Registered Historical Landmark, the building was renovated in the 1930s by John Nicholas Brown, and is undergoing another restoration by the same architects who oversaw the renewal of Trinity Church. It has served various purposes in its history, including town hall, theater, and art gallery. Plans now call for it be used as a museum and visitors' center.

Across Thames Street on the southwest corner of the square stands the ABRAHAM RODRIGUES RIVERA HOUSE, now Citizens Bank. Maker of spermaceti candles and slave trader, Rivera was one of the early Jewish merchants of Newport. The gambrel-roofed house was built c. 1740, enlarged in 1758, and in 1803 became a bank. Open during business hours.

Across the square, PETER BULIOD (PERRY) HOUSE, 29 Touro Street, c. 1755. This large, three-story house with imitation brick exterior has served as a bank, billet for French troops in the Revolution, and headquarters for the Salvation Army. Greatly altered in 1795 to house the Bank of Rhode Island, the house was purchased in 1818 by Commodore Oliver Hazard ("We have met the enemy . . .") Perry, the naval hero of Lake Erie, who lived in the house for several months. An early owner was Moses Seixas, one of Newport's first Jewish merchants, who, as Reader at Touro Synagogue, received George Washington's message pledging religious freedom.

JOSEPH AND ROBERT ROGERS HOUSE, 37 Touro Street, c. 1798. The large size of the house and its elaborate doorway, with fanlight leading to broken pediment, are typical of Federal transition-period architecture, when decoration and classical influences were becoming features of residential building. The house served for years as headquarters of the Preservation Society of Newport County.

Turning right on Clarke Street, named for one of Newport's founders, you will find the PELEG BARKER HOUSE, also

Three Walking Tours

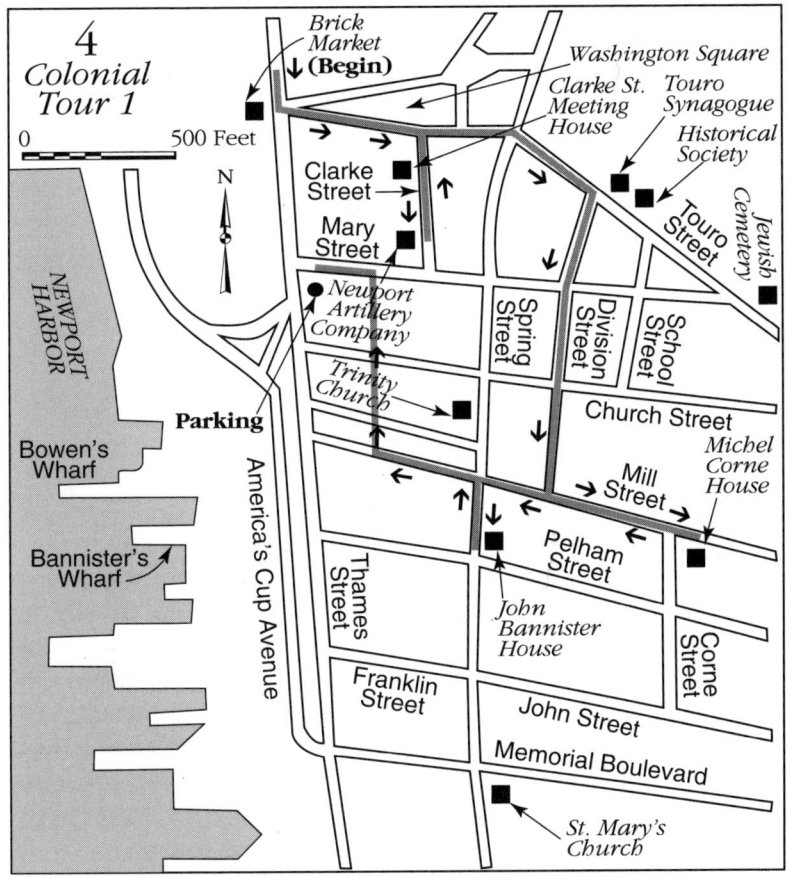

known as the Bell House, at 11 Clarke Street. Built about 1759, the house originally was two stories, but was raised to make room for a garage on the first floor. Peleg Barker taught the three Rs here in the 1780s, and his brother Matthew ran a blacksmith shop on the site. The house has been considerably altered, and has lost its center chimney and central doorway.

CLARKE STREET MEETING HOUSE (Second Congregational Church). Built in 1735 by Cotton Palmer, the church has been extensively remodeled. It was damaged while being used as a hospital by the British and French during the Revolution. In 1874 it was enlarged and the original tower was enclosed in a Greek Revival facade. The church played a major role in the intellectual and religious life of the colony and was a center for the anti-slavery movement here. A National Historic Place, the building has gone the way of many Newport dwellings—it's been converted to condos.

Next door is the NEWPORT ARTILLERY COMPANY at 23 Clarke Street. Built by the stonemason who built Fort Adams, this is the home of the oldest militia in continuous service in America (See Chapter 3—" Museums").

The ROBERT STEVENS HOUSE, 31 Clarke Street, c. 1750, housed several of General Rochambeau's aides during the French stay in Newport in 1780–81. Now a bed-and-breakfast.

The VERNON HOUSE, across the street on the corner of Clarke and Mary streets, was Rochambeau's headquarters during the Revolution. A National Historic Landmark, the house was built in the early 1700s and expanded to its present size in the 1750s by Metcalf Bowler, a merchant and supposed patriot who may have acted as a double agent for the British. William Vernon, an ardent patriot, rented the house from Bowler in 1772 and bought it two years later, but was forced to flee during the British occupation. Here Rochambeau met with Washington and Lafayette and laid plans for final victory at Yorktown. The impressive wooden house has a "rusticated" exterior, like the Redwood, in which the exterior walls were painted and sanded to resemble stone. One of the downstairs rooms contains Chinese-style paintings dating from the early 1700s that may have been inspired by a merchant's visit during the China Trade.

Heading back to Washington Square, on the east side of Clarke Street, is the RHOADES-PEASE HOUSE at No. 32. This blue colonial was built about 1700.

EZRA STILES HOUSE, 14 Clarke Street. A National Registered Historic Place, this house was built in 1756 as a parsonage for the Congregational Church opposite. Its most famous tenant was Ezra Stiles, historian, scientist, and minister here from 1775–76. Stiles was a friend of Benjamin Franklin and conducted some of the first electricity experiments in this area. He grew white mulberry trees in his garden and attempted to introduce the silkworm to Newport. His experiment with lightning rods was no more successful—shortly after he installed one on the Congregational Church, the roof caught fire. Stiles helped found Brown University, and later served as president of Yale University. An outspoken patriot, he was forced to leave Newport during the Revolution. The house was enlarged in 1834 when the Doric portico was added.

WILBUR ELLERY HOUSE, 51 Touro Street at the corner of Clarke Street. Built about 1800, this handsome brown house with white trim has been restored. It was the home of William Ellery III, son of one of the signers of the Declaration of Independence.

Turning right, cross Spring Street and continue up Touro Street to find the LEVI GALE HOUSE at 89 Touro on the corner of Division Street. This large Greek Revival house, that looks more like a temple than a home, was built between 1833–38 by Rhode Island architect Russell Warren for Gale, a wealthy New Orleans native. Note the flat roof, squarish lines, and two-story fluted Corinthian pilasters. The house once stood at the head of Washington Square where the courthouse is now, a fitting complement to Brick Market at the far end.

Turning into Division Street, you are entering one of the most historic byways in the city. Between Touro and Mill streets, you will pass a variety of fine period houses, dating from the early 1700s to the mid-1800s. Across from the Levi Gale house, on the northeast corner of Division, is the GIDEON CORNELL HOUSE, 3 Division Street. Although the plaque on the house says it was built in 1785, other sources date it as early as 1714. The fanlight doorway probably was a later addition.

A few steps away is the ELISHA GIBBS HOUSE, 5 Division Street, built c. 1745. Across the way at 20 Division Street is the DANIEL CARR HOUSE. The steep roof on this simple two-story red colonial is one indication that it was built early in the century (c. 1712).

At 37 Division Street, on the west side again, stands the NASSAU HASTIE HOUSE. Built c. 1760, it was owned by a barber and peruke maker (peruke was a French term for wig).

Crossing Mary Street and continuing on Division, you will find on the corner at 40 Division the AUGUSTUS LUCAS HOUSE, site of a colonial uprising. Built c. 1741 and later enlarged, the house had a number of notable inhabitants, including Augustus Lucas, a French Huguenot merchant and slave owner. His grandson, Augustus Johnston, was an attorney general and stampmaster, and it was in the latter capacity that he aroused the anger of local residents. When the Stamp Act was passed, an irate mob went to the house and Johnston was forced to hide in the cellar. He was saved when a friend promised the crowd he would resign as stampmaster. During the war French troops were quartered here, and in 1813–14 Commodore Oliver Hazard Perry made it his home.

Next door at 42 Division Street is the AILMAN HOUSE, a simple half-house c. 1748. Half-houses were a common colonial way of getting a roof up when money was short; when better times came, the second half could be built. The usual half-house plan was two large rooms and one small room on each floor.

The very colonial-looking house at 46 Division Street was built in 1751 and owned by Dr. Samuel Hopkins, pastor of the First Congregational Meeting House, abolitionist, and hero of Harriet Beecher Stowe's novel, *The Minister's Wooing*. Hopkins, with the aid of other early abolitionists like Ezra Stiles, convinced the General Assembly in 1774 to end the slave trade, the first such law in this country. This led to a total ban on slaveholding ten years later. Newport Gardner, a learned black man, was a deacon in his church.

Across the street at 49 Division is a nineteenth-century church converted to a house. Only the exterior retains authenticity.

The THOMAS GODDARD HOUSE, 78 Church Street (corner Church and Division), was built about 1800 and named for a member of the famous family of cabinet and furniture makers in Newport. Crossing Mill Street, take a look west toward the harbor. On the right day, when the harbor is filled with sailboat masts, you can imagine how Newport looked to those who lived here a hundred or two hundred years ago.

On this short stretch between Mary and Mill streets we find the WILLIAM CARD HOUSE at 73 Division Street, a typical three-quarter house built c. 1800. The three-quarter house contained one large room and two medium-sized on each floor.

The BILLY BOTTOMORE HOUSE, 70 Mill Street (corner of Division), retains the center chimney characteristic of houses built in the early 1700s.

To take a brief detour, turn left on Mill and walk up to the junction of Corne (pronounced Cor-nay) Street on the South side. The MICHEL FELICE CORNE HOUSE on the corner (No. 2 Corne) was home to the Italian painter, known for his War of 1812 battle scenes, and for perpetrating what was considered a bold act at the time. Aware that his American neighbors considered the tomato to be poisonous (and probably aware that the Indians had been happily eating them for years), Corne announced that he would publicly consume the fruit at high noon in Washington Square. He showed as promised and, in the presence of the curious crowd assembled there, ate not one tomato but several. Corne bought what was then a barn in 1822 and converted it to a two-story house with gable roof. The back ell is a later addition.

Follow Mill Street back down to Spring Street. You are now in the heart of the Historic Hill area, surrounded by colonial homes. The NORTON WILBOUR HOUSE, northeast corner of Spring and Mill streets, was built c. 1777 and is another example of a half-house with end chimney.

Turn left on Spring Street and continue to the corner of Pelham Street for the JOHN BANNISTER HOUSE, 56 Pelham Street. Built c. 1751, this was one of several houses owned by

Bannister, prominent merchant (and smuggler). The size of the gambrel-roofed, two-chimneyed dwelling is indicative of Bannister's success. Unpopular British general Prescott made this his headquarters during the occupation. (He would have saved himself an ignominious experience had he slept here every night—see Prescott Farm under "Area Attractions" in Chapter 3.) Reversing direction on Spring Street, there are a number of fine colonial specimens on the west side, including the JONATHAN GIBBS HOUSE at No. 181, a tiny two-roomed cottage that has been restored. Next door is the SAMUAL BOURS HOUSE, 175 Spring Street, a large three-story home built prior to 1777. The ALEXANDER JACK JR. HOUSE on the corner of Spring and Mill, recently restored, is a typical three-quarter house, built c. 1811. Standing on this busy corner, not far from the spring where the first Newport settlement was made, it is difficult to imagine that it was once sparsely populated. Between the early houses, there was much space and even some in-town farmland.

Turning left down Mill Street toward the harbor, there is an unbroken row of colonial homes beginning with the JOSEPH BEATTIE HOUSE at 47 Mill Street, built before 1758. At 41 Mill is the BERIAH BROWN HOUSE, a good example of an early farmhouse, with sections dating from the early 1700s. The house originally stood in North Kingstown, but was disassembled and floated across the bay, a not uncommon practice in earlier times when wood was scarce. Next to this is the BILLINGS-COGGESHALL HOUSE, a peculiar double house built c. 1784. Take a peek into the cobble-stoned courtyard. Until recently, Coggeshall House was headquarters for the Newport Restoration Foundation.

Cut back up the street a bit to the entrance of Goelet Park beside Trinity Church. This shady patch of green with its bubbling fountain is a good spot to take a few minutes' rest if you're inclined. Continuing through the park, you pass HONEYMAN HALL, named in honor of the church's first pastor, James Honeyman, done in Greek Revival style to complement

Trinity Church. TRINITY CHURCH, at the head of Queen Anne Square, is one of the most beautiful colonial churches in the country with a long and interesting history (see Chapter 2, "Major Sights"). Open to the public.

Turning down Church Street, you will find the ERASTUS PEASE HOUSE at No. 36. Built in 1785, the house has a curious gambrel roof curved at the eaves.

Next door is the DR. COTTON HOUSE, once one of a long row of merchant houses that lined Thames Street. It was moved to this site in the early 1980s to help complement Queen Anne Square. The gambrel with large central chimney was built before 1758. Dr. Cotton is remembered as having served as surgeon aboard the US *Constitution* ("Old Ironsides"). Completing the row is the JOHN LANGLEY HOUSE at No. 28, a gable roof with a nice fanlight door, built c. 1807. The current owner Elizabeth Meyer restored *Endeavour,* one of the few 1930s-era J-class boats extant, and the house serves as office for her company, J-class Management, Inc.

This tour has touched upon just some of the many historic homes and buildings within the Historic Hill district. If you wish to continue the tour on your own, you can walk up Pelham Street from Thames, or along Spring Street in either direction. Pelham Street, incidentally, was the first to be lit by gas lamps in this country. Appropriately, Newport's program to renew gas lighting began on the same street in the 1970s.

2. THE POINT

Time: Approximately an hour and a half. Parking: in one of the central city lots or anywhere near Washington Square or the Gateway Center. The trip can be divided up if the walk seems too much. There are also several parks with benches along the way.

The Point, originally called Easton's Point, has been described as one of the finest eighteenth-century neighborhoods

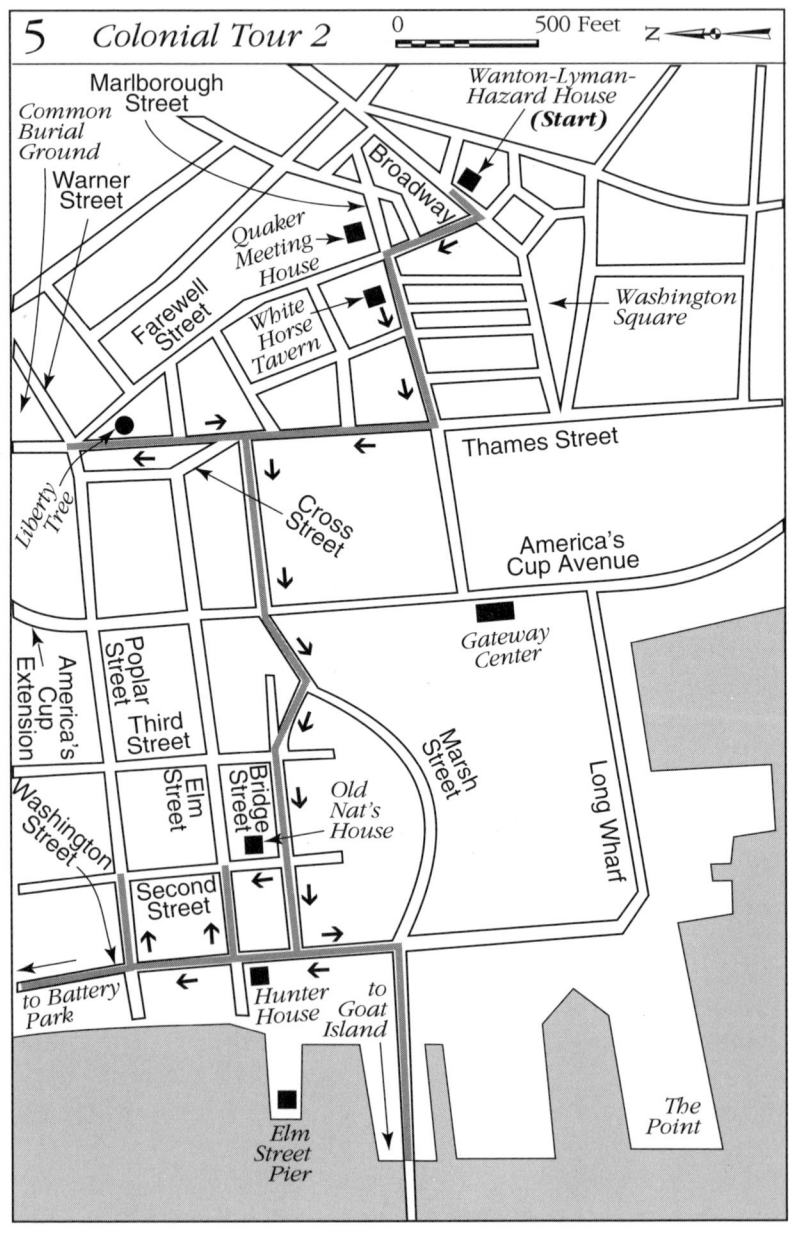

in the country. Despite some destruction by the British during the Revolution, the area has more than one hundred colonial homes, many of them restored. (Not all the destruction by British troops was vandalism; bitter cold winters forced the cut-off soldiers to tear down houses for firewood.) Interspersed with the historic dwellings, of course, are many houses of more modern construction.

Geographically, the Point is defined as that area north of Long Wharf and west of Thames Street running along the inner harbor. Until 1725 it was a quiet, rural area with just a few houses and shops going up along upper Thames Street. In 1725 a prominent Quaker family, the Eastons, bought up most of the area and began selling off lots. The first group of residents settled in along Bridge Street, then named Shipwright Street after the ship's carpenters who lived and worked there. They were joined by members of the Townsend and Goddard families, who were famous for their high-quality furniture. The next sizable group to move in was composed of sea captains, who moored their ships off Washington Street and built docks for the loading and unloading of goods. The captains built a series of impressive homes along Washington Street and up Bridge Street. By 1800, there were 21 sea captains living on Bridge Street alone.

Before getting to the Point proper, there are several buildings worth viewing on Marlborough Street, one block north of Washington Square. At the northeast corner of Marlborough and Farewell (so named for the cemeteries that line the road) is the QUAKER MEETING HOUSE, dating from the eighteenth century. Open to the public (see "Churches" in Chapter 3).

On the opposite corner of Farewell and Marlborough stands the WHITE HORSE TAVERN, believed to be the oldest tavern in America. One of the city's oldest structures, the tavern was built before 1673. The pirate William Mayes obtained the first liquor license in 1687, and the sign of the White Horse was hung out by Jonathan Nichols in 1730. Taverns often served as public meeting places; the town council, and possibly the General Assembly, met here. A school for girls was held on the premises as well, run by Miss Matilda Nichols. The tavern has its original center chimney and has been carefully restored by the Preservation Society. Operated as one of Newport's finer (and most expensive) restaurants, the White Horse is open to the public.

ST. PAUL'S METHODIST CHURCH on Marlborough Street was built in 1806 and is said to be the oldest Methodist Church in the world to have a steeple and bell. Open for services and on weekend mornings for visitors.

Continue west on Marlborough to the corner of Thames to CODDINGTON HOUSE, 2 Marlborough Street. Built c. 1730, the house was owned by Governor John Coddington. The shell doorway is a copy of one made for the house in 1737 by famous colonial carver John Stevens.

Turn right onto upper Thames. The JONATHAN ALMY HOUSE, 73 Thames, was built about 1750. Next door, the

Colonial houses on Pelham Street, the first street to be lit by gas lamps in this country.

RICHARDSON PECKHAM HOUSE at No. 67, built c. 1740, has an unusual hip-style roof with center chimney.

The EBENEZER HATHAWAY HOUSE, 57 Thames, was built in Assonet, Massachusetts about 1707 and moved here. The CAPTAIN WILLIAM READ HOUSE on the east side at 58 Thames is a gambrel-roofed home built end-to-street to save lot space. Built c. 1730. Captain Read was a leader of the Sons of Liberty opposed to the Stamp Act.

A few doors up is the JEREMIAH LAWTON HOUSE, 52 Thames, built c. 1740. Across the street is the brown-painted WILDER HOUSE at 53–55 Thames, built in 1730 as a farmhouse and moved here from across Narragansett Bay.

Cross Bridge Street for a moment and continue up Thames. The large red house at 44 Thames is the JOB BENNETT HOUSE, owned by a Tory who was forced to flee when his allegiance to the crown was discovered. The roof is a good example of the gable-on-hip style. Bennett placed a mark on the large chimney that identified him as a loyalist to the British aboard ship in the harbor but couldn't be seen by his neighbors.

The three-story gambrel-roofed house at 36 Thames is another example of building end-to-street to save space. Built before 1750, the recessed doorway with sidelights probably is a later addition.

The JOHN STEVENS HOUSE, 30 Thames, was built in 1709 by the noted stonecarver, who had his shop across the street. It was enlarged in 1750 as Stevens's business flourished. The JOHN STEVENS SHOP at 29 Thames was one of the earliest businesses in the country. Founded in 1705, it describes itself as the "oldest marble works" in America. Examples of Stevens's work can be found in the various colonial cemeteries around town. In 1927, John Howard Benson, artist, writer, and stonecutter, took over the business from the last of the Stevens family. Benson's work is exhibited in many of the country's leading museums. After President Kennedy was killed in 1963, Benson's son Fud Benson received the commission to carve the memorial to the late president at Arlington Cemetery. Several generations of Bensons continue the craft to this day.

If you wish, you can walk up Thames to the junction of Farewell Street and see the LIBERTY TREE, planted by the Sons of Liberty to symbolize opposition to the Stamp Act and, ultimately, British rule. The British cut the tree down when they arrived in 1776, but it was replanted when they left several years later. The present tree, a fern-leaf beech, was planted and rededicated in 1897.

One block farther on Farewell brings you to the COMMON BURYING GROUND. The large red house at the corner of Warner and Farewell streets, known as the COZZENS HOUSE, was built c. 1760 and is a good example of a double house—two separate houses inside one skin, with two front doors and two chimneys.

The burial ground, once well beyond the city limits, started as several distinct cemeteries, the south side for freemen, the north for slaves. Of the 3,000 or so stones here, about 800 date from the 1600s to before 1800. Among them are some excellent examples of colonial gravestone carvings. The adjacent ISLAND CEMETERY, with an entrance on Warner Street, is notable for its monuments to the Perry brothers and the *Standing Angel* by Augustus Saint-Gaudens, a major sculptor of the late nineteenth century.

Doubling back on Thames to Bridge Street, you will pass a small park with several stone benches and a plaque designating the entire district as a Registered National Historic Landmark.

The first building on the right at 3 Bridge Street is the JOSEPH STEVENS HOUSE, or the Penny Post House, built before 1750. Across the street at 6 Bridge Street is the BENJAMIN HOWLAND HOUSE, a modest gambrel-roofed farmhouse built c. 1720 and moved here from Dartmouth, Massachusetts.

The WILLIAM CLAGGETT HOUSE, 16 Bridge Street, was owned by Newport's famous clockmaker. You can see one of his clocks in the Sabbatarian Meeting House at the Newport Historical Society, still ticking away after more than 200 years.

Claggett, like Ezra Stiles, was a dabbler in mechanical curiosities, including electrical devices. In 1747, a Boston newspaper reported that the clockmaker was in town to demonstrate "the new Method of Electrifying several Persons at the same time, so that Fire shall dart from all Parts of their Bodies." The proceeds, at 10 shillings a head, were donated to charity. His house was built c. 1718.

The CALEB CLAGGETT HOUSE, 22 Bridge Street, was owned by William's father, who was given the property by his son and built the house c. 1725. The JAMES GARDNER HOUSE, 23 Bridge Street, was built c. 1750. The little gambrel was inhabited by Gardner, a goldsmith, until the 1790s.

One of Newport's great love scandals is attached to the CAPTAIN PETER SIMON HOUSE at 25 Bridge Street. According to the story, dancing master Peter Simon Jr. secretly married one of his pupils, Hannah Robinson, against the wishes of her Quaker father, who owned a large plantation across the bay in South County. She was disowned and the strain took its toll on Hannah's health. When the dancing master abandoned his now penniless bride, she took ill and died. She was buried beside the family house in South County, and Peter was barred from the funeral. The house was built c. 1727 and is typical of the sea captains' houses that once lined the street.

The DOUGLAS CAMPBELL HOUSE, 31 Bridge Street, also known as the Southwick House, was built in 1750 and moved here from another site in Newport. Campbell was a cabinetmaker. Note the beautiful scallop shell doorway.

You must now cross the America's Cup Avenue extension, built in the 1970s to connect downtown Newport with the Newport Bridge. Unfortunately, it also cut the Point section in half and forced the removal of some houses.

The GARDNER TOWNSEND HOUSE, 53 Bridge Street, was built c. 1735 and is typical of the smaller gambrel-roofed houses of the period.

The JOHN PAIN HOUSE, 10 Third Street, on the southwest corner of Bridge, is a good example of a roughly built colonial home. Note the crooked panes over the door. Built c. 1750, the house once served as a pewter shop and was repaired after the Revolution. In all, Bridge Street lost about 17 houses to British destruction, so the number of fine homes still standing is remarkable.

The MARTHA PITMAN HOUSE, 59 Bridge Street, was built c. 1758 as a shop or barn and converted to living quarters about 1800. It was brought here from another site.

The JOB (JOHN) TOWNSEND HOUSE, 70–72 Bridge Street, was one of many homes owned by the cabinet-making Townsends in the Point area. As many as 14 members of the family were engaged in the work and, with their in-laws the Goddards, they created many museum-quality pieces. John Townsend owned the house and an attached workshop in 1792, but the building probably dates to before 1740.

The large blue gambrel on the north side of the street is the SHERMAN CLARKE HOUSE built c. 1783. Note the pineapples carved above the doorpost. The pineapple, symbol of hospitality, was often displayed when captains were back from the sea and the family was receiving visitors. There's some suspicion the pineapple also was employed on occasion to warn shoreside lovers that the master of the house was about.

Looking to the right up Second Street, you will see a small blue gambrel-roof with (crooked) center chimney dating from 1717. Known as OLD NAT'S HOUSE, it was moved here in 1969.

CHRISTOPHER TOWNSEND HOUSE and STUDIO, 74–76 Bridge Street, was the first house in the Townsend complex. Christopher was a ship's cabinetmaker. The house was built c. 1725 and has a gable-on-hip roof.

The stately building that reigns over the west end of the street is the PITT'S HEAD TAVERN, a popular colonial coffee house. It was built before 1726 by Henry Collins, well known as a patron of the arts. Ebenezer Flagg enlarged it to its present size in 1744. The house, which at that time stood near Washington Square, housed both British and French troops during the

Revolution and became a tavern after the war. Owner Robert Lillibridge named his tavern after William Pitt, British prime minister and libertarian. It was moved to No. 77 in 1966.

The JONATHAN JAMES HOUSE, a three-story gambrel built before 1775, finishes out Bridge Street. The large house at the south corner of Bridge and Washington Streets is the BRENTON COUNTING HOUSE, No. 39, which stood on Champlin's Wharf downtown and provided offices for early merchants. It was built in 1748. Like many of the houses on the street, it is on the National Register of Historic Places.

Proceeding north, there is the GEORGE TOPHAM HOUSE at 41 Washington Street, built in the mid-eighteenth century. Prominent Rhode Islanders Joseph Tillinghast and William Cranston lived here.

Across the street at 54 Washington stands the HUNTER HOUSE, a National Historic Landmark, considered to be one of the finest examples of colonial residential architecture in existence (see Chapter 2, "Major Sights"). Well worth a visit.

The large red three-story gambrel at 62 Washington Street is the CAPTAIN JOHN WARREN HOUSE, built about 1736. Captain Warren is believed to have enlarged it about 1774, putting in a central hallway and two chimneys, but it has changed little since then.

The QUAKER (TOM) ROBINSON HOUSE, 64 Washington Street, has been owned by a single family for more than 200 years. It was headquarters for Vicomte de Noailles from 1780–81. The earliest part of the long house dates back to 1725. Quaker Tom bought it in 1760 and built an addition on the north, changing the original two-story building to the large three-story gambrel of today.

Unusual for the area, the SANFORD COVELL HOUSE, 72 Washington Street, stands where the John Goddard house once was located. The large Victorian, with a fine back porch and view of the harbor, now operates as a bed-and-breakfast.

This is the end of Tour 2, but you can continue to wander the streets of the Point, discovering more fine examples of colonial architecture. A little farther up Washington Street is Blue Rocks (officially Battery Park), a pleasant place to sit and look out over the harbor. Elm and Poplar Streets, which run at right angles to Washington, are particularly pleasant thoroughfares. To get back to your starting point, you can walk up Elm to Cross Street, which leads to Thames, or follow Second or Third Streets south to Bridge and take a left.

3. VICTORIAN HOUSES

The neighborhoods around the Redwood Library offer a cross-section of some of the most important architectural styles of the mid- to late-nineteenth century, when American designers were searching for their own look. Some of the results were overly cute "cots," laced with excessive trimmings; some buildings are a mishmash of conflicting ideas, while others are simply elegant houses.

A number of artists and writers have made their homes in this area over the years. Architects Richard Morris Hunt and George Champlin Mason both designed and built their own homes here. This tour, which should last no longer than an hour, can be combined with a visit to the Redwood Library, the Newport Art Museum, or Touro Park with its old stone tower. You can park anywhere in the Redwood Library area, or even walk up from downtown if you like. This is a quieter, unhurried part of the city with many lovely homes along the way.

You can begin the tour with the SAMUEL PRATT HOUSE, almost directly across Bellevue Avenue from the Redwood and tucked between two commercial buildings. Although there is no hard evidence that Richard Hunt designed this dwelling (also known as Bird's Nest Cottage), the shape of the gable is similar to that on his own house, designed about the same time (1870–71). Note the colored slates that sheathe the house. With its decorative towers and fancy lace under the eaves, the house

Three Walking Tours

6 *Victorian Tour 3*

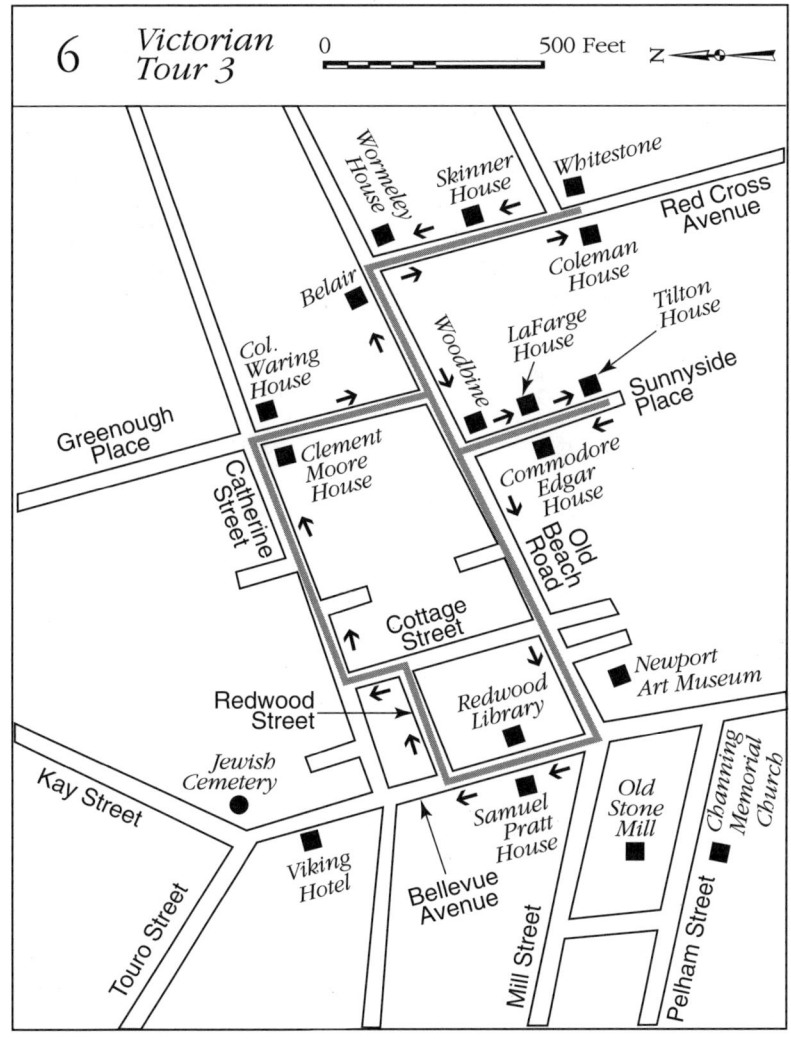

The Samuel Pratt house, also known as Bird's Nest Cottage.

may be considered to border (or cross the border) on quaintness. A "rustic" fence that once extended across the front is no more. The building now houses a real estate office, so go inside, if inclined, and note the functional simplicity of the interior.

Walking the length of Redwood Street past the library will bring you to a T-intersection with Cottage Street. The house to the left, on the northwest corner, is a typical Gothic-style cottage with high gables and the cruciform shape common to Victorian homes. The house was built in 1846. Turning left onto Cottage, then right on Catherine Street, walk two blocks to the CLEMENT C. MOORE HOUSE at 35 Catherine Street. It would be nice to report, as local stories have it, that this rambling Victorian got its name because the Rev. Moore was inspired to compose his famous poem, "A Visit From St. Nicholas" ("The Night Before Christmas"), here while spending a lonely Christmas away from his family. In fact, the poem was written in 1822 in New York State and the house not built until 1850. Moore spent summers here later in his life.

Across Greenough Place, on the corner of Catherine, is the COLONEL GEORGE WARING HOUSE at 33 Greenough Place. Built by Richard Hunt for his own use, the house is a curious hodgepodge of styles—hints of colonial symmetry, a touch of European chalet in the gables, and a taste of the classical in the columns that mark the front entrance. The roof is a combination of gambrel and hip rather than the peaked Gothic kind found in the Redwood Street house, for example. For Hunt, who experimented with stick-style wooden houses earlier in his career and marble palaces later, the house he later sold to George Waring is a muted departure.

Walking right (south) on Greenough Place, you will come to Old Beach Road, the pathway that Newporters took to the beaches below before Memorial Boulevard was built. A left will take you up half a block to Red Cross Avenue. Before crossing to Redwood, take a look at the house on the north side of Old Beach, known as Belair. The large house, now apartments, was built in 1870 in what was called the Tuscan revival style. Also visible are the gatekeeper's cottage and stables in the same style.

At 2 Red Cross Avenue on the corner of Old Beach is the KATHERINE PRESCOTT WORMELEY HOUSE, built in 1876–77 as a summer residence in the blossoming neighborhood. Charles McKim of McKim, Mead and White gave the house elements of the stick style and a Tudor influence as well. The onion-domed tower was probably McKim's "romantic notion of a residence" at the time, according to Newport architect John K. Grosvenor, who lives next door.

The turreted house at 6 Red Cross is the SKINNER HOUSE, designed by McKim, Mead and White in 1882. The tower and shingled exterior are reminiscent of the same firm's Newport Casino, built two years earlier. Overall, the architectural elements are more harmonious than in the earlier Wormeley House.

WHITESTONE, the large house at the corner of Red Cross and Oakwood Terrace has an unusual pebbled exterior, but is otherwise typical of the colonial revival houses of the late 1800s. The dormers, columns, and cornice in the classical style give it the institutional look of a college building (it's an apartment building).

Across the street, the SAMUEL COLEMAN HOUSE at No. 7 is a colonial revival that looks distinctly American. It has the shingle look typical of McKim, Mead and White, who built it in 1882, but a definite colonial gambrel roof.

Returning to Old Beach Road, take a left and continue to WOODBINE, the yellow chalet at the corner of Sunnyside Place. Here George Champlin Mason, best known as an architectural historian and author of the book *Newport and Its Cottages,* outdid some of his more famous contemporaries, creating a pleasant house that's a basic Swiss chalet shape with broad projecting eaves and white trim that enhances rather than overwhelms. Mason called it his "model cottage" and it's conceivable that Hunt decided to sell his house after he saw what Mason had built for himself just a block away.

Sunnyside Place is a short street with several interesting houses. The large estate that dominates the west side is the COMMODORE EDGAR HOUSE, a brick mansion designed by McKim, Meade and White in 1885–86. As much a Tudor mansion as anything else, the house now serves as a retreat for corporate executives.

The white house at 10 Sunnyside is most remarkable for being the primary residence of artist John La Farge after 1873. La Farge was a landscape painter best known for his beautiful stained glass windows. He arrived in Newport in 1859 after a stint in Europe where he studied painting with William Morris Hunt, the architect's artist brother. Other students included William and Henry James and Thomas Sergeant Perry, a grandson of Commodore Oliver Hazard Perry. He fell in love with Perry's sister, Margaret, and despite religious differences (he was Catholic, she Episcopalian), they were able to marry. Her money bought the house on Sunnyside Place, which remained in the family until 1956.

At the end of the street on the left is the SAMUEL TILTON HOUSE, 12 Sunnyside Place, yet another McKim, Mead and White design, dating from 1881–82. This is a stylish house, with its large windows and plaster surface embedded with glass— more successful in its modest way than the mansion across the street.

You can complete the tour by one of several routes. You can return west on Old Beach Road to Bellevue Avenue, flanked on the left by Hunt's Griswold House, now the Newport Art Museum, and the pleasant grounds of the Redwood Library on the right. Or you can continue down Mill Street, directly ahead, where there are several fine Greek Revival and Federal houses, or cross the park to Pelham Street, where there are several intricately carved Victorian dwellings and a row of stately Greek Revival homes leading down to Spring Street.

5
TOURS OUT OF TOWN

✨✨✨✨

HERE ARE THREE SHORT TOURS that will take you out of Newport for part of a day. The first is through Tiverton and Little Compton in the easternmost part of the state. It's a pleasant ride that should take between two and four hours, depending on how many stops you make. The second tour is a variation on the first—instead of heading south to Little Compton, you go north to Fall River, the small Massachusetts city just over the Rhode Island line.

The third tour is of neighboring Jamestown, second largest island after Aquidneck and with a bit of history of its own. This is a shorter outing, but it does entail paying the toll each way on the Newport Bridge. (Hint: Although not strictly legal, you can purchase bridge tokens for $1 at some stores in Newport and Jamestown instead of paying $2 at the bridge.)

Tours Out of Town

1. TIVERTON AND SAKONNET

To get to Tiverton, once part of the Massachusetts Bay Colony, drive north on Aquidneck, following RI 138 to the Sakonnet River Bridge. Take the first exit on the bridge (if you miss it, don't panic, just take the next exit) and follow Main Road down the hill. Take any one of several lefts (Lawton Avenue in particular) up the hill to Highland Avenue. FORT BARTON, the first attraction, rises up above the street across from Town Hall. Park your car and walk up the blacktop path to the heights above. Fort Barton was hastily erected in 1777 in response to the British capture of Newport. Named for Colonel William Barton who kidnapped General Prescott (see "Prescott Farm," Chapter 3), the fort was really an earthworks with some timber support. However, from its height 110 feet above the Sakonnet River, its guns held a sweeping command of the north end of Aquidneck. The fort was the jumping-off place for the attack on Aquidneck in 1777, a move that, but for the defection of the French fleet at a crucial moment, might have ended the war in its second year. Today, the fort has been partially restored, three miles of hiking trails put in, and a lookout built that will give you a good view of the northern end of Aquidneck Island and surrounding waters.

Return to Main Road (RI 77), either by going back down the hill or by driving south on Highland Avenue, and follow it south for several miles through rural Tiverton. At 3119 Main Road, on the left, you'll notice a two-chimney house set back a bit. This is the ABRAHAM BROWN HOUSE, later called the Adoniram Brown House. Lafayette stayed here during a stopover in Tiverton in 1778.

At 3622 West Main Road, on your right, is the CAPTAIN ROBERT GRAY HOUSE, birthplace in 1775 of the man who skippered the first American ship to sail around the world (1780–90). Captain Gray also discovered the entrance to the Columbia River, giving the United States a convincing claim to the Pacific Northwest. He died at sea of yellow fever in 1806.

7 Newport County Tours 1 & 2

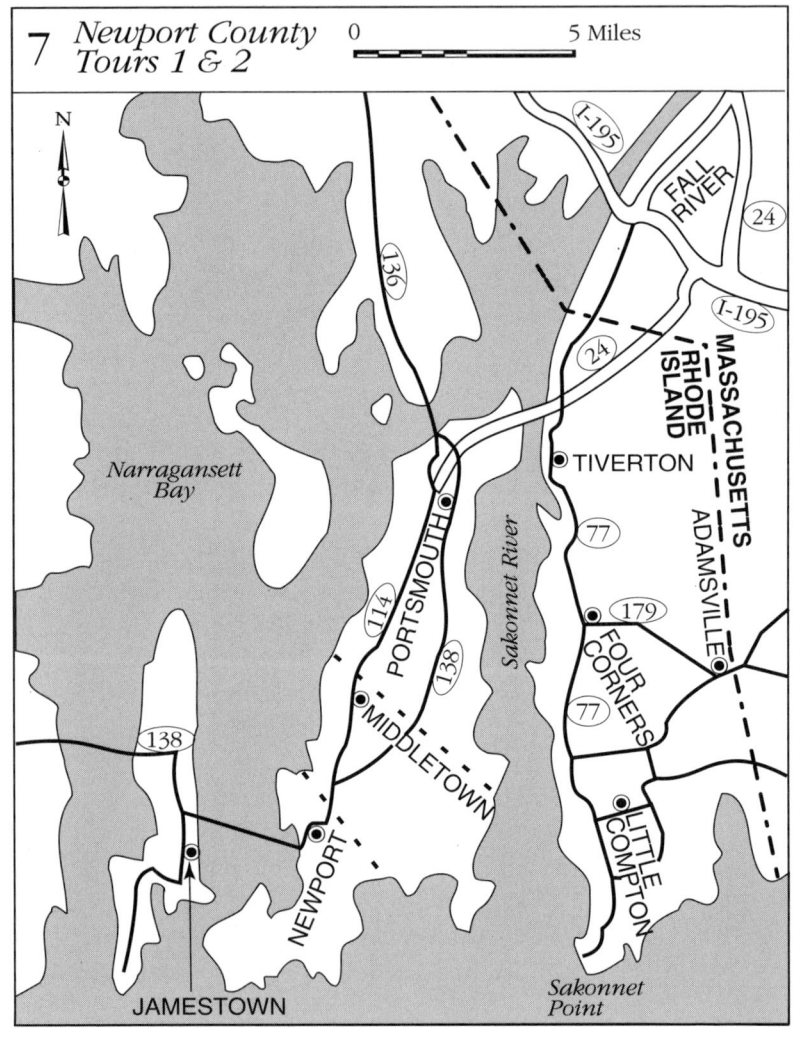

Half a mile up the road is Tiverton Four Corners, where there are several notable structures. The stately yellow house on the near left is the SOULE-SEABURY HOUSE, built in 1760 by Abner Soule, whaler, blacksmith, and soldier. His son, Cornelius Soule, enlarged the house in 1809, but in 1816 was forced to deed it to Cornelius Seabury, merchant and farmer, for payment of a debt. Once open as a museum, the building, unfortunately, was sold some years ago along with all its original furnishings. But don't be surprised if you see an ancient mariner comfortably seated on the stone wall outside—some local residents swear they've seen the spirit of Abner Soule returned to his former homestead.

The building across the street, on the northwest corner of the intersection, was for years the A. P. WHITE STORE, built as a country general store in 1875. It now houses Provender's, an upscale (and excellent) gourmet food store. The late Victorian structure has a high mansard roof and cupola. Original proprietor Andrew Peregrine White was postmaster, ice cutter, dry-goods supplier, and social director for this section of Tiverton for many years.

The little store diagonally across the intersection, Gray's Ice Cream, is famous locally for its ice cream, and there's likely to be a crowded parking lot and a long line on summer weekends. An even better ice cream, in the opinion of some, can be found a few miles farther down RI 179, East Road. Take a right at the fork onto Stone Church Road; pass the Old Stone Church (built back to front so the congregation could keep watch for hostile Indians) and continue down the long grade into the village of Adamsville. Simmons' Variety claims its ice cream has the highest butter fat content in the state and thus the best taste. There's a small bench outside where you can sit and enjoy your ice cream. The large white private house across the street was home to the Von Trapp family for years after it fled the Nazis in Austria.

Continuing south on RI 77, the little gambrel-roofed house just a tenth of a mile beyond the four corners is the CHASE-

CORY HOUSE, dating back to 1730, possibly earlier. The simple five-room house has its original kitchen and a seven-foot fireplace with beaded chimney. Donated to the Tiverton Historical Society by former Navy Secretary J. William Middendorf, the house is open to the public on Sunday afternoons 2–4:30 from the end of May through September, or by appointment (624-8881).

Three miles south of the Four Corners is SAKONNET VINEYARDS, on the left at 162 West Main Road, shortly after you cross the line into Little Compton and ascend Windmill Hill. The original owners, who built the vineyard in the 1970s, said they searched all over before selecting this spot, which most closely resembled the climate of Burgundy. This is not just a regional winery—some of the vintages have won national prizes. Offers tours, slide show and wine tastings Wednesdays, Saturdays and Sundays from May 1 through October. Slide show and tasting other times. Free. For information call 635-8486.

A few miles farther south, you cross the line into Little Compton, or Sakonnet (Place of the Black Geese to the Indians). Little Compton was settled in 1674 by members of the Plymouth Colony. It was one of five towns turned over to Rhode Island in 1746 by royal decree.

Take a left at the sign pointing to Little Compton Center for a look at an almost perfect survivor of the typical New England village. The graveyard dividing Little Compton Common was laid out in 1675 and contains the body of Elizabeth Pabodie, daughter of John ("Speak for yourself") and Priscilla Alden, as well as that of Benjamin Church, the Indian fighter who in 1676 put an end to King Philip's War that had ravaged the colony. The graceful church is the United Congregational Church, built in 1832 to replace an earlier house of worship, and enlarged in 1872–74. This was the congregation that respectfully declined to allow the makers of the movie *Witches of Eastwick* to film their church interior.

About a mile down West Main Road you come to the WILBOUR HOUSE, also open to the public. The original two-story, two-room section dates from 1680. You can tell it by its low ceilings and exposed corner posts. Rooms were added in the eighteenth and nineteenth centuries, but the house retains its simple quality. Restored in 1956 under the direction of the Little Compton Historical Society, the house contains seventeenth- and eighteenth-century furniture. There's also a display of antique farming and household equipment in an adjoining barn. Open mid-June to mid-September on Tuesdays through Saturdays from 2–5 p.m. Admission $2.50 adults, 75 cents for children.

Returning to West Main Road, you can either retrace your drive or continue south to Sakonnet Point, the easternmost point of Rhode Island where there's a breakwater you can walk out on and a superb ocean view.

2. FALL RIVER

Maybe Fall River, Massachusetts, can't boast of George Washington, Oliver and Matthew Perry, or the Vanderbilts, but it is the hometown of the world's most famous ax murderess, Lizzie Borden. The city that once ranked second only to Manchester, England as a cotton producer, with more than 120 mills in operation, has now become famous for its discount factory outlets. Tour buses go to Newport for the mansions; you'll see tour buses here, too, but the passengers are intent on shopping.

The mill outlets, complexes of stores set in old cotton mills, are concentrated along Quarry, Alden, and Queque-chan (Quick-a-shan, if you need directions) streets, not far from MA 24 and I-195 (Brayton Avenue and Plymouth Avenue exits, respectively). There are some not-so-great deals lurking here, but also some real quality at real bargain prices. For information, including maps, write or call the Fall River Factory Outlet District Association, P.O. Box 2877, Fall River, MA 02722 (508-678-6033).

The LIZZIE BORDEN HOUSE, 234 Second Street, opposite the bus station and one block up from Main Street, is virtually unchanged from the steamy August morning in 1892 when someone chopped up Lizzie's stepmother and father. Because Lizzie was acquitted (although circumstantial evidence strongly points to her guilt), the case has been the source of endless speculation since that August 4 day, as well as the subject of numerous books, a play, a movie, and even a ballet. An annex housing the Leary Press is attached to the north corner of the house that once led to the side door and the barn where Lizzie claimed to have taken refuge from the heat, munching on peaches while someone axed her parents. Other than that, the house is eerily the same, although the current owners strongly protect their privacy and allow no one in. From the street you can see the upstairs bedroom window (left front) where Mrs. Borden was unpleasantly surprised while making up the guest bed.

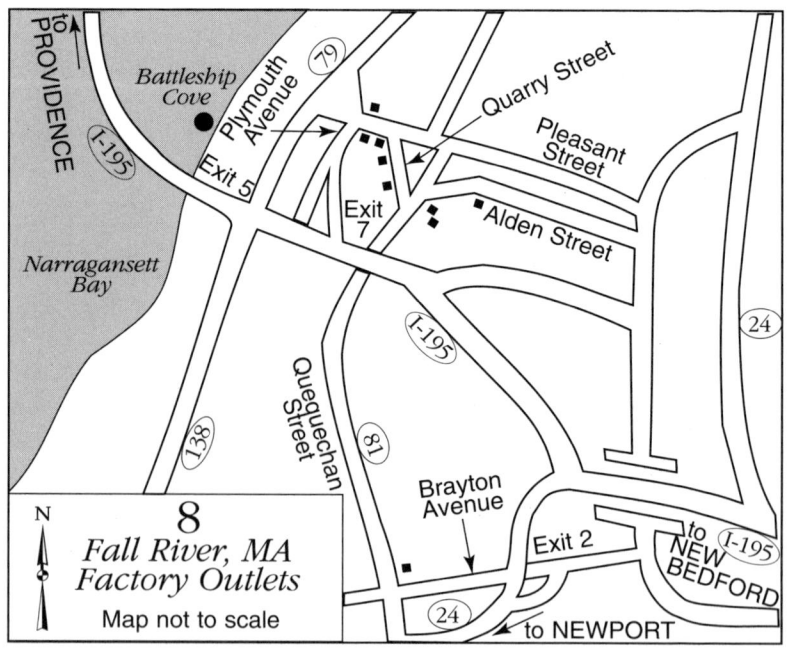

Those wishing to learn more about Lizzie can visit the FALL RIVER HISTORICAL SOCIETY, 451 Rock Street (508-679-1071), which houses the physical evidence from Lizzie's trial, including a bloody bedspread, an ax—apparently not the murder weapon, which was never found—and other memorabilia, including a Japanese fairy tale about the peculiar Victorian who lived out her last years in seclusion. Hours: 9 a.m. to 4 p.m. Tuesday through Friday, all year. Open weekends 1–5 p.m. June, July, and August. $3 for adults, $1.50 for children 10–17.

MARINE MUSEUM AT FALL RIVER, 70 Water Street (508-674-3533). On the Fall River waterfront, straight down from downtown, in the shadow of Braga Bridge (I-195). Known for its *Titanic* exhibit which includes a 28-foot model of the doomed liner, nine cases of artifacts from the ship, an audio from a survivor, and a video of the discovery of the ship by scientists from Woods Hole Oceanographic Institute. Also an excellent history, with models, photos, and artifacts, of the Old Fall River Line, the steamboat service that linked Fall River, Newport, and New York from 1847 to 1937. Besides passengers, the line carried cotton and cotton goods to and from the city, at one time the second largest cotton mill town in the world. Open 9 a.m. to 4:30 p.m. weekdays, 10–5 Saturdays and Sundays all year. Admission is $3 for adults, $2 for children.

BATTLESHIP COVE, at Fall River Pier on Davol Street, just north of Marine Museum (508-678-1100). Centerpiece is the battleship *Massachusetts* ("Big Mamie"), the 680-foot battleship that saw action in the Atlantic and Pacific theaters in World War II. Other boats open for tours include the destroyer Joseph P. Kennedy, Jr., the World War II attack submarine Lionfish, and PT boats 796 and 617, two of the speedy plywood torpedo boats that harassed the Japanese Navy. Open 9 a.m. to 4:30 p.m. daily year-round, except for Thanksgiving, Christmas and New Year's. Admission is $8 for adults, $4 for children from 6–14; ticket stub good for admission to the Marine Museum.

Note: While in Fall River, you might want to sample some of the Portuguese/Azorean cuisine—excellent tasting dishes at about half what you'd pay for a comparable meal in Newport. Two of the better ethnic restaurants are T. A. (Tabac Acoreana) Restaurant at 408 South Main Street, near downtown, and Sagres at 177 Columbia Street, between Main and Davol, in the heart of the restored Portuguese district. As a bonus, Sagres on weekends offers fado singers with your supper.

3. JAMESTOWN

The large island just to the west of Newport is Jamestown, or Conanicut (named for Narragansett sachem Quononoquitt). It was bought in 1656 by William Coddington, Benedict Arnold, and several others from Newport, incorporated as a town in 1678, and named in honor of King James II. Many of the early settlers were Quaker farmers and shepherds. The island's strategic location at the mouth of Narragansett Bay was recognized early, and it was fortified by the colonists in 1776. The British stormed the island in December of 1776, burned many of the buildings, and took up occupation until the French allies of the colonists landed in 1778. The island was bombarded frequently by the British during the war, and the islanders in turn took potshots at the British ships in the harbor.

When you come off Newport Bridge, which replaced a ferry connection in the 1960s, drive north on RI 138 and bear left at the traffic island about one mile up the road. At the traffic signal (the only one on the island) turn left onto the North Road. About one-half mile down, on the right, is WATSON FARM, a working farm that is open to the public and particularly fun for children to visit. The 280-acre farm, that dates back to the mid-1700s, has sheep, horses, and black angus cattle. Watson farm is owned by the Society for the Protection of New England Antiquities, and members of the amiable caretaker family are happy to explain its operations. The farm is open Tuesday, Thursday, and Sunday between June 1 and October 1 from 1 to 5 p.m. Free admission, but donations are accepted.

Tours Out of Town 107

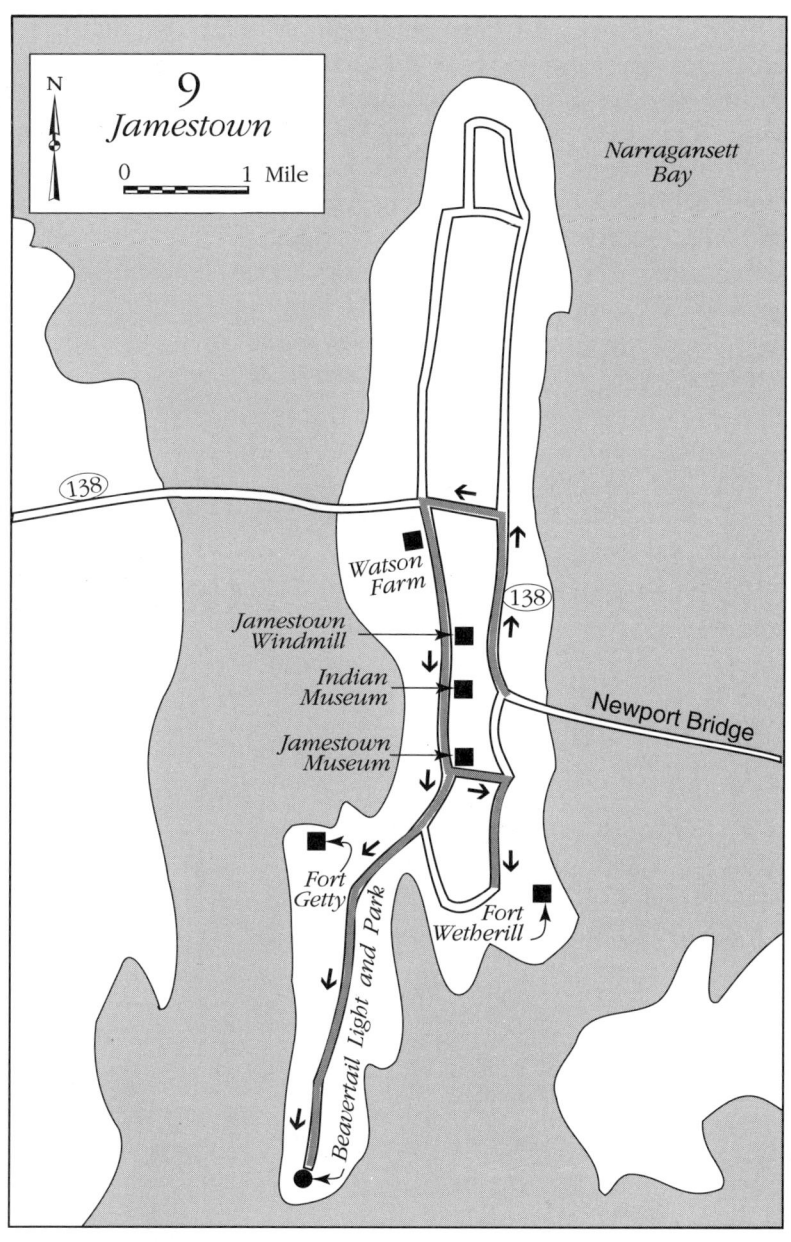

Turn right from the farm and continue south another one-half mile to the intersection of Weeden Road. There, behind the Quaker meeting house, stands the JAMESTOWN WINDMILL, which operated between 1789 and 1896. Restored by the Jamestown Historical Society, the mill is open to the public Saturday and Sunday mid-June to Labor Day from 1 to 4 p.m. The mill, called a smock mill for its appearance, is based on a popular English design of the sixteenth and seventeenth centuries. Rhode Island once was dotted with them, but this is the last in working condition. Inside, you can view the gears, the stone for corn grinding, and the granary. No admission charge, but donations are welcome.

A mile farther south, you will reach the public library, site of the SINDNEY L. WRIGHT MUSEUM. Indian artifacts from prehistoric to colonial times are on display. Jamestown was inhabited by the Narragansett tribe, who used the island as a summer camp, when the Europeans arrived. Archaeologists are still researching the many centuries of Indian life on the island. Open during library hours. Call 423-2665.

Continue south along North Road until you meet the flashing light at the intersection of Narragansett Avenue, the town's main thoroughfare. Take a left. The JAMESTOWN MUSEUM (423-0784) at 92 Narragansett has memorabilia from the 300-year-old Jamestown ferry system, the island's only link to Newport until the Newport Bridge opened (still a traumatic event for islanders on both sides) in 1969. Other Jamestown historical items. Open Tuesday to Saturday from early June to Labor Day. Small fee.

The JAMESTOWN FIRE MEMORIAL, also on Narragansett Avenue, has an interesting display of the town's early firefighting equipment, including a horse-drawn pumper. Open Tuesday to Saturday 9 a.m.–4 p.m.

Retrace your path on Narragansett Avenue to the North Road intersection. Take a left on what is now Southwest Avenue and follow it around the town beach to Beavertail Road. At the very end of the road (and the island) is the BEAVERTAIL

LIGHT, one of the oldest lighthouses on the Atlantic Coast (the original was built in 1749). The 1938 hurricane uncovered the base of the oldest portion, and you can see an example of early colonial stonework. The present granite tower was built in 1856 just north of the first site. The Beavertail light was used for a number of experiments during the nineteenth century, especially to develop new and better fog horns. There's an excellent view of the ocean from the point, and the area is noted for its fishing.

Follow your trail back around the coastline to the east branch of East Shore Road. This leads to FORT WETHERILL on Ocean Street. The fort, set on the highest point of the island, overlooks the so-called East Passage of Narragansett Bay (some feel the Sakonnet River is the true East Passage and not a river at all). The first fortication here was Fort Dumpling, built in 1776. The federal government built Fort Wetherill later, parts of which remain. Most of the area is in the wild and it's a good place for hiking, picnicking, and just plain viewing. You can pick out Newport's Trinity Church to the east, Point Judith and the outline of Block Island to the south. Somewhere down along the shore is where Captain Kidd, who stayed here with friend and fellow pirate Thomas Paine in 1699, supposedly buried his treasure before going off to Boston, where he was arrested. He was taken to England, tried and hanged, and his reputed treasure was never found.

6
WHERE TO STAY

EXCEPT FOR A BRIEF PERIOD during the 1800s, Newport has never been a hotel-style resort—that is, until now. Earlier visitors either had society connections—and a place to stay with friends—or they built their own summer cottages. A recent building boom, including the 317-room Marriott Hotel on Long Wharf, has greatly increased the number of rooms in the city, but space remains tight on the busiest summer weekends. Last-minute visitors who haven't booked ahead sometimes have been forced to look for a bed as far away as Providence or the Connecticut border.

Nor are rooms in the larger hotels cheap by any standards—in peak season you'll pay as much as in Washington, D.C. or New York. Usually that means $150 and up for starters, $200 or more for a room with a water view. Rooms with the euphemistic "island" or "city" view generally are less. Fortunately, a cottage industry—literally—of bed-and-breakfast operations and smaller inns has sprung up, offering alternative, often cheaper places to spend the night. According to a *USA Today* survey, Newport County has more B&B's and inns than anywhere in the country. And there's always the old traveler's standby, the motel or motor inn where prices dip below $100, especially as you move away from the city into Middletown or Portsmouth.

HOTELS

Newport Marriott, Long Wharf/America's Cup Avenue, adjacent to the Gateway Center (849-1000; toll-free reservation number, 1-800-228-9290). The Marriott, opened in 1988, is the city's newest as well as largest hotel. Peak-season rates (May 12 to September 14) range from $179 to $219. The hotel has an impressive five-story atrium as you enter, two restaurants, a lounge with a Top-40 DJ, indoor pool, and a health club with sauna for guests' use. Racquetball courts, for a small fee. In summer, an oyster bar is activated. The Marriott also has a good central location, on the harbor and close to downtown and the wharf areas.

Newport Harbor Hotel & Marina (formerly Treadway), on the harbor (847-9000; reservations, 1-800-955-2558). In a city where names can sometimes be deceptive, the Harbor Hotel is indeed right on the harbor. It's also downtown and close to the wharf action. Summer rates (Memorial Day to Labor Day) range from $160–$210, depending on day of the week and whether there's a view of the harbor. Fall and spring rates are $120–$180, cheaper in winter. Two- and three-day packages are also available ($359–$549), offering breakfast, one dinner, and mansion tickets. Restaurant and nightclub offer relaxed jazz and comedy nights.

Doubletree Inn (formerly SHERATON ISLANDER), on Goat Island (849-2600). The second largest of Newport's hotels, with 253 rooms, Doubletree's first hotel in the Northeast is a bit removed from the hustle of the city, which is the way many guests prefer it. Excellent views of the harbor and bay. In-season rates are $155 for landside view room, $175 for water view, and $210 for a balcony overlooking Narragansett Bay. Guests over the years have included President Gerald Ford and King Hussein of Jordan. Doubletree is a short, pleasant walk across the causeway to the Point section, or you can make use of the hotel's shuttle van. Several restaurants and lounges.

Hotel Viking, 1 Bellevue Avenue, at the top of Touro Street and Historic Hill (847-3300). Slightly apart, in one of the pleasanter sections of town, the Viking is still within reasonable walking distance of downtown and the waterfront. The Viking was once the queen of Newport hotels, the largest in the city until the newer buildings on the waterfront; the original colonial-style building is on the National Historic Register. Some of the waterside rooms have spectacular harbor panoramas. June through August rates are $159/room. There's an outside patio and a small jazz bar where Ella Fitzgerald has sung. Thornton Wilder stayed here while he wrote his Newport book, *Theophilus North*.

INNS AND BED-AND-BREAKFASTS

For those who don't require or want the full services of a hotel, a stay at an inn or guest house can give a sense of what it was like to have lived in Newport in bygone eras. Accommodations range from what is termed a "homestay," a night in a private home renting one or two rooms, to smaller "inns" or guest houses with five to nine rooms, to full-fledged inns with 15 or 20 rooms and some of the amenities you'd find in a hotel or motel. Some places require a minimum two-night stay during peak season; many have no-smoking rules. Although generally less expensive than hotels, inns and bed-and-breakfasts aren't necessarily cheap: rates can range from $50–$60 a night for a room with a shared bath to $150 or more, with the average during summer about $100. There are several helpful (free) reservation

Where to Stay

services that will match you with the best choice or, when space is tight, find you a spare room. The services also inspect their clients' places and certify them according to national association standards. By the way, you'll always get breakfast with your bed in an official bed-and-breakfast, though it may be just a light Continental meal of rolls or muffins and coffee.

Anna's Victorian Connection (849-2489) is one of the more established services, with 100 or so bed-and-breakfast and guest home listings. Offers accommodations of all types—the "Victorian" in the name refers to the owners' own homes.

Bed & Breakfast of Rhode Island (849-1298), 38 Bellevue Avenue. Service owner Rod Wakefield hopes also to offer package deals, under the name Tour Newport, that will provide discounts to restaurants and tourist attractions for service users.

Bed & Breakfast Newport (846-5408). Owner Cindy Roberts has about 55 clients, ranging from one or two rooms in a colonial house to the more contemporary 40-room Greenhouse Inn near the beach in Middletown.

Harbor Boat & Breakfast (207-871-0208). If you'd prefer to spend the night on a boat instead of dry land, this service by Beth and Jeff Rand in Maine will find you accommodations on a variety of vessels, from a 28-foot Sabre to a 44-foot Gulfstar. Prices range from $120 to $200, depending on the boat.

There probably are hundreds of inns and guest houses of varying size in the Newport area. Given our own prejudices (we prefer quiet to centrally located), here are a few that we would recommend, although there are certainly others worth visiting.

Francis Malbone House, 392 Thames Street (846-0392). A beautifully restored and furnished Georgian colonial (c. 1760), the Francis Malbone House was chosen one of the country's 10 best in 1990 by *Inn Business Review,* a national trade publication. There are 10 rooms on three floors, including a suite in an adjoining wing that once served as a counting house. All the rooms have private baths, and six have working fireplaces.

There are three elegant sitting rooms on the first floor and a breakfast room with full hearth. In warmer weather you can take your breakfast outside to the garden terrace. The rooms are furnished with Queen Anne period reproductions and queen-size four-poster beds. Although you're on busy Thames Street in the heart of the waterfront district, this solid house offers a calm and quiet atmosphere. Rooms range in price from $125 (garden view) to $155 (harbor view) from May 1 to October 31; $80 and $95, respectively, off-season.

Admiral Fitzroy Inn, 398 Thames, next door to Francis Malbone House (846-8361) Full-fledged inn with 18 rooms located in a former convent. Summer rates are $125–$145, includes cable TV, full breakfast, private parking. Beautifully painted rooms furnished with either brass or European-style sleigh beds.

La Forge Cottages, 96 Pelham Street (847-4400). A sturdy Victorian located near Touro Park, La Forge combines convenient location with just enough peace and quiet. There are no "cottages"—the name dates back to the turn of the century when Madeline La Forge and her husband Philip opened a rooming house and began buying area homes to expand their business. The current bed-and-breakfast, run by Dutch couple Margo and Louis Droual, has eight rooms and four suites, one with balcony. The rooms have private baths, TV, small refrigerators, and telephones. A full breakfast is delivered to your room each day. Summer rates are $75–$95 for a room, $95–$125 for a suite. Winter rates are $50–$75.

Ivy Lodge, 12 Clay Street, off Bellevue Avenue, bordering the mansion district (849-6865). This large Victorian, or "small mansion," as the owners call it, was designed by Stanford White and built as a summer home in 1886. Ivy Lodge's location puts you within easy reach of the mansions—The Elms is a block away—and also provides the gift of quiet surroundings. Outside, there's a wraparound porch for catching summer breezes; inside, you'll find an oak-paneled entry that rises 33 feet and a regal staircase with hand-turned balusters. There are 10 guest rooms on three floors, eight with bath. Each room is different, but there's lots of chintz, Laura Ashley, and wicker to convey the overall feel of a summer house. Since the host is a chef, guests are treated to a full breakfast. Rates from April 1 to November 1 range from $95 to $150 a night, depending on the room (one comes with jacuzzi).

Victorian Ladies, 63 Memorial Boulevard, near the Cliff Walk (849-9960). Several bed-and-breakfast owners we know picked Victorian Ladies as one place they'd like to spend a weekend. Nine rooms, all with bath, are split between the main house, an 1841 Victorian, and a carriage house, reached via a latticed courtyard. All the rooms are done differently in "subtle" Victorian, according to the operators. On a busy thoroughfare (to the beaches) but sufficiently insulated from traffic noises. Full breakfast, parking. Summer rates to $140, off-season about $85.

Cliffside Inn, 2 Seaview Avenue, off Cliff Avenue (847-1811). Another Victorian (c. 1880) in a nice, quiet location above the Cliff Walk. Screened porch and lots of trees. Built as a summer cottage for Governor Thomas Swann of Maryland and later owned by Newport portraitist Beatrice Turner, the inn has 12 antique-furnished rooms, all with bath. Full breakfast and hors d'oeuvres at 5:30 each afternoon. May 1 to November 1 rates $115–$185; off-season rates $85–$155.

Jailhouse Inn, 13 Marlborough Street, one block from Washington Square (847-4638). Housed in the former county jail (c. 1772) and Newport police station, the Jailhouse Inn now serves voluntary inmates. Just the same, the windows are barred and the jail motif is carried out in the black-and-white striped bed linen. Continental breakfast. Summer rates (June to September) are $105–$115 weekdays, $115–$125 weekends; $55 and $65 off-season.

Sanford Covell House, 72 Washington Street (847-0206). The location of this bright blue Victorian house, looking over Newport Harbor to the west, makes it one of the city's popular inns.

There's a backyard heated saltwater pool, jacuzzi, and large wraparound porch. Five Victorian-appointed rooms and two apartments; summer rates $95–$225, depending on size, location, and private bath.

Mill Street Inn, 75 Mill Street, on Historic Hill (849-9500). Halfway between the waterfront and Bellevue Avenue, the inn features contemporary rooms, all suites, in a restored sawmill built in 1815. Parking in an underground garage, Continental breakfast, wet bars, refrigerators. Summer rates range from $165–$195; $75–$95 off-season.

Rhode Island House, 77 Rhode Island Avenue (849-7765). In a quiet neighborhood near the center of the Kay Street Victorian neighborhood, Rhode Island House is an 1883 Victorian done in muted Queen Anne decor. Five rooms, four with nonworking fireplaces, two with jacuzzi. There are working fireplaces downstairs and the overall "getaway" atmosphere tends to attract a younger, thirties crowd. "Extended" Continental breakfast. Two-night minimum on weekends, three on holidays. Summer rates $140 and $160 (depending on jacuzzi); $75 and $100 off-season.

Inn at Castle Hill, Ocean Avenue (849-3800). The small mansion was built in 1877 for Professor Alexander Agassiz, naturalist and geologist, who chose the castle-shaped point of land as the ideal place for his marine laboratory. He built his house on a crest of a hill with a sweeping view of the ocean and his laboratory at the foot, facing the harbor. The main house contains 10 rooms, seven with private bath and ocean view. Nearby are six harbor house rooms, all with bath. Guests have the use of a private beach. Rates June through October are $180 for rooms with bath, $80 for the smaller rooms with shared bath. Harbor house units are $115.

Castle Hill also operates an excellent restaurant, serving a classic menu (lobster, lamb steaks, Dover sole) in a richly paneled room lined with fireplaces. Jackets are required. Prices $25 and up.

Hydrangea House, 16 Bellevue Avenue (846-4435). Centrally located (across from the Viking Hotel), but surprisingly calm. Five nicely finished rooms, all decorated with original art (there's a gallery downstairs) and all with private bath. Entries in the guestbook compliment the food (full breakfast), the decor, the hospitality, and the peace and quiet. A deck out back overlooks a flower garden and, of course, hydrangea bushes. No phones, no TV—this is a getaway spot—but there is a phone in the upstairs lobby. Off-street parking. Rooms $115–$125 in-season, from May–October.

Brinley Victorian Inn, 23 Brinley Street, off Kay Street (849-7645). Tucked away on a side street but still close to Bellevue Avenue and downtown, Brinley consists of 17 rooms in two separate 1800s structures. There are porches for lounging on and a brick courtyard between the buildings where a Continental breakfast is served in warm weather. The inn, which is AAA-approved, won the *Yankee Magazine* Apple Pie Award several years ago, and we heard innkeeper Peter Carlisle telling guests about his 800-calorie blueberry muffins. Again, no TV or telephones in the rooms, but the library has a phone where local calls are free. Off-street parking. Prices range from $95–$130 in summer, with off-season packages, including bargain dinners locally and mansion tickets, available.

Finnegan's Inn at Shadow Lawn, 120 Miantonomi Avenue, Middletown (847-0902). In Middletown, but not all that far from downtown, Finnegan's is a stately Victorian manor fronted by an expansive lawn. The main house (c. 1853) has eight guest rooms on the second and third floors; the first floor has a dining room and parlor. There are three more rooms out back in what once was a children's playhouse, and a single room in the former stables. All rooms come with TV, small refrigerator, and coffee for breakfast. Summer prices are $105 plus tax. To get to the inn, follow Broadway (RI 114) out of town to the stoplight at One Mile Corner. Take a right onto Miantonomi Avenue; the inn is at the first four-way stop.

Whimsey Cottage, 42 Briarwood Avenue, Middletown (841-5824). A smaller "homestay" arrangement—two rooms only—in a Victorian house near the beaches. Owner-operator Joanne Moody describes her house as "nostalgic," filled with antiques, dolls, even a toy train. The second-floor rooms, both with ocean view, rent for $85 a night in season and come with a "hearty Continental" breakfast and the personal attention expected in smaller B&Bs.

Flag Quarters, 54 Malbone Road (849-4543). Somewhat off the beaten track in the north end of the city, Flag Quarters (one of the owners is a Navy captain) is another smaller homestay B&B with two suites on the third floor. The Victorian-style suites ($95 in summer, $65 winter) come with private bath, cable TV, microwaves and refrigerators, and a separate entrance for those wishing privacy. Breakfast is left outside your door mornings and announced with a china bell.

If you don't mind the potential noise and congestion of staying downtown, here are several more stopovers in the heart of the city, all with good reputations.

Admiral Benbow Inn, 93 Pelham Street, 15 rooms with private bath (846-4256).

Admiral Farragut Inn, 31 Clarke Street, eight rooms with private bath (846-4256).

Queen Anne Inn, 16 Clarke Street, 12 rooms, some shared baths (846-5676).

Bannister's Wharf, West Pelham Street, five rooms, three suites either on the wharf or overlooking the busy marina (846-4500).

MOTELS AND MOTOR LODGES

Best Western Mainstay Inn, 151 Admiral Kalbfus Road, across from Newport Jai Alai (849-9880; reservations, 1-800-528-1234). 113 rooms. Peak season rates are $88 weekdays, $98 weekends (off-season, $40). AAA, corporate and AARP discounts. Sunday afternoon the local Friends of Jazz bring in regional and national talent for just a few dollars cover charge.

Howard Johnson Lodge, 351 West Main Road, Middle-town, near Two Mile Corner (849-2000; for reservations, 1-800-654-2000). 155 rooms, pool, tennis courts. July–September rates $115–$119; off-season $45–$85.

Journey's End Motels, 249 Connell Highway, near the Navy Base (848-0600; for reservations, 1-800-668-4200). No-frills accommodations in 80 units. June 1 to September 5 rates $63.88, one person, $71.88 for two; off-season, $48.88 for one, $56.88 for two.

Newport Courtyard, 9 Commerce Drive, just off RI 114, about two miles from town (849-8000; reservations, 1-800-321-2211). Marriott's no-frills lodging for business travelers doesn't offer room service, but there is a restaurant, lounge, and pool on the premises. 148 rooms. Peak-season rates $119; $79 off-season. Ten suites at $149 in-season, $109 off.

Budget Motor Inn, 1185 West Main Road (RI 114), about three miles from town (849-4700). The rooms are cheap, the amenities few, but this is where much of the cast and crew stayed during the making of the film *Mr. North* (based on Thornton Wilder's book about Newport) in 1987. 77 rooms at $90.50 from Memorial Day through October; $32.50 in spring, closed in winter.

Royal Plaza, 425 East Main Road, several miles from town (846-3555). New hotel with 48 rooms, restaurant, and lounge. July and August $98–115 weekdays, $115–130 weekends; much lower off-season.

Sea View Motel, Aquidneck Avenue, Middletown, on a hill overlooking the beaches (847-0110). Forty rooms, all with ocean view. Coffee shop. Late May to September 30 rates $65 weekdays, $75 weekends.

CAMPGROUNDS

Paradise Mobile Home Park, 459 Aquidneck Avenue, Middletown (847-1500). Close—about one mile—to area beaches and town. Self-contained units only, with a maximum length of 30 feet. Full hookups, but no pets, please. Price: $20 per night.

Meadowlark Trailer Park, 132 Prospect Avenue, Middletown (846-9455), has 40 sites with full hookups, several with only electricity. Dumping station, but no bathrooms or showers. $20 for two people.

Melville Ponds Campground, off RI 114 (West Main Road) in Portsmouth (849-8212). On a hill overlooking the West Shore, Melville has 34 sites for RVs with full hookups, $20/day, 31 with water and electricity at $16/day, and about 50 tent sites for $13/day.

Second Beach Family Campground, Second Beach, Middletown has about 10 transient trailer sites (another 50 are rented seasonally or monthly) with water and electrical hookups. Restrooms available. Campsites located between Second and Third beaches. Reservations required (call 849-2822). Fee is $22/night and $140/week. Season runs from mid-June to Labor Day.

Fort Getty Recreation Area, Beavertail Road, Jamestown (423-1363). The largest campground in the area, Fort Getty has seasonal sites for 100 trailers and about 25 tents. Water and electrical hookups; no sewage, but there is a dumping station. Fee for trailers is $20/night, $15 for tents. Season runs from Memorial Day weekend to mid-October (Columbus Day).

For more information on camping in Rhode Island, there's a toll-free line, 1-800-556-2484, good throughout the U.S. and Canada. Within Rhode Island, the number is 277-2601, or you can write the Rhode Island Department of Economic Development, One Weybosset Hill, Providence, RI 02903.

7
DINING IN NEWPORT

🙢🙢🙢🙢

YOU CAN EAT OUT VERY WELL in Newport, thanks to the French and *Homarus americanus*—which shows how far the taste of local residents has come in the last two hundred years.

At one time, incredible as it seems, *Homarus americanus,* or the Maine lobster, was considered throwaway food, fit only for bait or the tables of poor families. To serve it to a guest would have been considered an insult. Happily, it was discovered somewhere along the line that lobster ranks with any food known to man, and fortunately Rhode Island and nearby ocean waters abound with the creatures.

As for the French, they've made quite a comeback since the days of the British occupation. The British may have been the enemy, but they shared the same language, religion and culture as the majority of Americans. Before they retreated, they solemnly warned the colonists that their supposed allies the French not only worshipped the Pope, they also ate—can you imagine—snails and frogs' legs. Well, Newporters were famous for their religious tolerance (although the General Assembly had to hastily okay the presence of Roman Catholics, the only religious group not permitted in the colony), and the first French masses in America were celebrated in 1780–81 at the Colony House in Washington Square. And it wasn't long before French cooking caught on. Today, the best restaurants in the city all serve French cuisine.

You can dine here well for moderate amounts of money, or you can spend a lot. The following list of restaurants, which is by no means complete, is grouped loosely by price, but there is much crossover. The first category contains four of the best, which are also among the most expensive. (Some, however, have begun serving lower-priced "bistro" meals to keep customer levels up.) The next group is moderate to expensive, where you can expect to pay $10 to $15 for many entrees. In the inexpensive category, there are some good restaurants where you can eat well for under $10.

Lobster is the great equalizer, of course. No matter where you order it, expect to pay in the expensive category, although you will find a difference of $5 to $10 between restaurants. Because lobster prices are in constant flux, many places do not list the price on their regular menus. Ask the waiter or waitress. And watch the extras. An appetizer and dessert can double the cost of a meal. In some places, dinner comes with salad and vegetable, while in others everything costs extra. Most Newport restaurants now post their menus outside the door so you can make your comparisons without going in. But don't be fooled by a full house—the food might be great or it may be packed with unsuspecting out-of-towners. With a little care, though, you should be able to have a memorable meal every night you spend in Newport. Note: hours vary, but many restaurants continue to serve until at least 10 p.m., often 11, during the summer season.

Four of the Best

Black Pearl, Bannister's Wharf (846-5264). Named for former owner Barclay Warburton's hermaphrodite brig, the Black Pearl is one of the class restaurants of Newport. The cuisine is French and the setting colonial. The Pearl began as a tavern in a former boathouse and sail loft, gradually emphasizing the food end of the business. The back dining room opened in the late 1960s, and the Pearl soon became one of the best-known restaurants in the area.

To get to the Pearl, you must negotiate the thick crowds (in summer) on Bannister's Wharf. You enter into the Tavern, the less expensive dining room, where you can get a cup of excellent chowder for $2.50 and a Pearl burger on Syrian bread with mint salad for $5.95. Entrees aren't cheap, just less expensive than in the adjoining Commodore's Room. There's grilled shrimp or

The Black Pearl outdoor cafe, Banniste's Wharf.

swordfish for about $16, or grey sole for $15.50. All dishes are slightly less at lunch. This is a rustic, comfortable setting, somewhat informal and a pleasant dining experience in its own right.

The Commodore's Room is a dress-up affair offering such appetizers as oysters with truffles and escargot (both about $7.50), and entrees such as filet mignon, breast of pheasant, and salmon steak. Expect to pay $20 and up for most dishes with the exception of the 2.5-pound grilled or steamed lobster, which goes for $35. Extensive wine list.

Across the wharf, the Pearl Annex consists of an outdoor bar and café, serving lighter meals at harborside. A very popular spot in summer.

Clarke Cooke House, Bannister's Wharf (849-2900). Along with its next-door neighbor, the Pearl, the Cooke House ranks with the area's best-known restaurants. Here again, the cuisine is French.

Clarke Cooke House on Bannister's Wharf offers fine dining and also houses the Candy Store, one of Newport's hot late-night spots.

The restaurant is part of a multifloor complex known collectively as the Candy Store, which houses the famous Daisy discotheque in the basement and the Sky Bar overlooking the harbor. The main restaurant is on the third floor of the restored colonial, dating from the 1790s and moved here from its original site on Thames Street.

If anything, dinner here is slightly more expensive than next door, about $25, but worth it. Dishes include salmon in sage sauce, roast lamb, and lobster sauteed in the shell in a sherry sauce with scallion cream. Many of the items are fresh from the owner's farm, Farmlands, in Portsmouth. Award-winning wine list.

One floor below, in the Bistro, entrees are simpler and less expensive—$10 for chicken fricassee in puff pastry, $12.50 for fettucine with shrimps and scallops. Afterward, you can have a drink from any one of several bars and watch the summer show that is Newport pass by.

White Horse Tavern, corner Marlborough and Farewell streets (849-3600). Definitely what Arthur Frommer would term a Big Splurge, the White Horse is one of the most formal and expensive places to eat in Newport. The setting, in the oldest tavern in America, is colonial, with candle-lit atmosphere Entrees run from $21 to $34 and the average couple can expect to spend a minimum of $60—the maximum can reach the hundreds. The White Horse offers a regional menu, with both seafood and meat. But the big three entrees are beef Wellington, rack of lamb, and Chateaubriand. Before, after, or in lieu of, dinner, you can relax in the comfortable fireplace bar where patriots no doubt once conspired to overthrow British rule over tankards of cider.

La Petite Auberge, 19 Charles Street, between Washington Square and Marlborough Street (849-6669). French dishes in the classic tradition—no nouvelle cuisine here—prepared by Chef Roger Putier, who has called himself "an ambassador of French cooking." Dinner (jackets required) is served in five intimate dining rooms on two floors of a colonial house once owned by Stephen Decatur, a naval hero ("Our country, right or wrong . . .") of the War of 1812 and the war against the Barbary pirates.

Putier is a native of Lyons, France, and apprenticed himself to a local restaurant at the age of 13. There he learned to clean pots, peel potatoes and chop parsley. Finally he was permitted to cook—for the dog. After cooking in the Lyons area and then Paris, Putier spent three years at the Élysée Palace as maître d'hotel in President Charles de Gaulle's private apartment. Now he does all his cooking at La Petite Auberge, considered by many to be one of the finest French restaurants for miles around.

Escargots, with a sauce of French mushrooms, poisson du jour flambé with Pernod, and le Wellington with truffle sauce—everthing on the *Menu à la carte* is distinctly French. Entrees cost from $18 to $30 dollars, but you can spend much more. The owner has made one concession to his locale; some fine California vintages have been added to the excellent wine list. There's also a bistro menu, served in an open-air café in warm weather, enclosed the rest of the year. Here, the menu relies heavily on grilled fish, steak, quail, and such. There's also a small but popular outdoor café in summer.

MODERATE TO EXPENSIVE

Le Bistro, Bowen's Wharf (849-7778). French country food in one of the best restaurants in Newport. Le Bistro's dining room is one floor up in a modern setting on busy Bowen's Wharf. Imaginative dishes in light sauces, but no minimalist cuisine—just satisfying meals. There's Filet of Sole Meunère ($12.95) and Grilled Veal Steak with leeks and mushrooms ($21.95), as well as basic Burgundian sausage with hot potato salad, and bouillabaisse. On the third floor there's a tiny bar with a harbor view where you can dine as well.

Christie's, on the harbor at 351 Thames (847-5400), has long been a favorite year-round with Newporters. One of the original waterfront spots, Christie's has a large busy bar and an informal, relaxed dining room. You can order steak or prime rib, but the main attraction is seafood—fresh lobster and the popular Narragansett Seafood Pie. The walls are adorned with yachting mementos and photographs of famous customers, including Elizabeth Taylor, Walter Cronkite and Van Johnson (a Rhode Island native). In the summer, Christie's Landing becomes an outdoor bar, with live music and a great view of the harbor and yachts. It's in easy walking distance of downtown.

The Pier, West Howard Street, on the harbor (847-3645). Often mentioned in the same breath as Christie's, The Pier is another old standby on the Newport waterfront. Again seafood is the specialty, and there's usually fresh swordfish on the menu. Three kinds of chowder: lobster bisque, clam chowder, which is thick and milky, and fish chowder, from a blackfish recipe concocted by pirate Tom Tew before the Revolution. Family dining in close quarters and live music in the adjoining lounge. Across Howard Wharf is what remains of William & Manchester Shipyard, where many America's Cup 12-meters were berthed.

Sea Fare Inn, 3352 East Main Road, Portsmouth, at the far end of Aquidneck (683-0577). Winner of numerous culinary awards, the Sea Fare offers fine food in a restored 1887 Victorian house. Owner-chef George Karousos says he follows the tenets of Archestratios, a famous chef in ancient Greece. By this he means using fresh (no marinating or freezing) foods in season, presented simply. That translates into such dishes as Chicken à la Grecque, Steak au Poivre, and swordfish stuffed with crab and lobster meat. The dining rooms are pleasant, and the food plentiful as well as excellent—worth the drive.

Star Clipper Dinner Train (849-7550, or 1-800-462-7452) offers something a little different—dinner on the Old Colony railroad train as you move (slowly, about 10 m.p.h.) along the West Shore of Aquidneck. This is a dress-up affair and costs about $50 per person, excluding drinks and tip. For that, you get a four-course dinner with a choice of three entrees—normally seafood, prime rib, and the chef's choice of chicken, veal or lamb. Dinner, served in two cars (the kitchen occupies the middle car), takes about three hours; on the trip out, beginning at 7 p.m., there's enough light to enjoy the view of Narragansett Bay. Floodlights highlight the scenery on the return trip. It may not be the Orient Express, but it's as close as you'll come in these parts.

Andrew's Restaurant, 909 East Main Road, Middletown (848-5153). Out of town also, but just a few miles, Andrew's is worth a visit for its imaginative, consistently high-quality food. Owner-chef Andrew Gold produces dishes like peppered sea scallops in a garlic cream sauce, marinated sirloin with peppercorn butter, and chicken Diablo that's *really* diablo. If you come for lunch, you can visit the adjacent Vinland Wine Cellars and sample some locally grown wines.

Scales & Shells, 527 Thames (846-3474). For seafood lovers only, but you'll probably love the seafood you get at this bustling informal restaurant on Lower Thames. It's one big room with the kitchen grills open for all to see. The menu is on a big blackboard on one wall. Mesquite grilled shrimp ($14.95) is moist and tasty; little neck clams or mussels in marinara ($11.95) are equally good. Salads, pasta with white or red sauce, and vegetable kebabs come with the meal or as side dishes. No fried seafood platters here. Terms are cash only—no credit cards.

The Mooring, Sayer's Wharf, off America's Cup Avenue (846-2260). Meat and seafood done in straightforward style in this old Victorian structure that once served as the New York Yacht Club's summer station. Great view of the center of the harbor from inside the restaurant and on the outside decks. Validated parking. Very popular in summer. Dinner $15 and up.

Dave & Eddie's (849-5241) at the south end of Brick Market Place, between Thames Street and America's Cup Avenue. Dave & Eddie's serves veal and steak, but seafood is the specialty—

lobster thermidor, seafood brochette, pasta with shrimp, and broccoli with garlic and oil and many more. Prices range from $12 to $20. Contemporary setting; semi-casual.

The Rhumb Line, 62 Bridge Street (849-6950). Set in the colonial Point neighborhood, a block and a half from the Gateway Center, The Rhumb Line (nautical for a direct line between two points) is a quiet haven away from the commercial area. Warm, inviting atmosphere. Known among locals for its mussels, fish, and veal dishes, as well as sandwiches and daily specials.

Chart House Restaurant, Bowen's Wharf (849-7555). Chart Houses are known for their excellent locations, and Newport's is no exception. Glass walls downstairs look directly out on cobblestoned Bowen's Wharf. Inside, the planked walls give the impression of being on a yacht. The harbor view from upstairs is one of the best in the city. Limited menu of steak and seafood, with chicken and steak teriyaki perennial favorites. So are the margaritas.

Muriel's, corner of Spring and Touro (849-7780), is a cozy, dimly lit restaurant at the head of Washington Square. Muriel's boasts of its prize-winning seafood chowder, but the main dishes ranging from broiled flounder or sole to filet mignon, with several vegetable dishes, are good and moderately priced as well. Prices range from $9 to $17. BYOB.

Puerini's, 24 Memorial Boulevard, near Bellevue Avenue. Very popular with locals, Puerini's dining rooms fill up fast in the warmer months. Homemade pasta in many varieties at reasonable prices. BYOB, and no smoking, please. No credit cards. Upstairs, there's a pasta shop for those who want to bring some additional Puerini's home.

La Forge Casino, 186 Bellevue Avenue, is a Newport institution, with mainstream meat and seafood dishes. The Porch dining room overlooks the greens of the adjoining Newport casino, offering a breath of spring even in the cold weather. The Casino Room is a turn-of-the-century restaurant *cum* Irish pub, with lots of sandwiches and pub dinners such as Dublin

Shrimp. A small but strategically located sidewalk café overlooks the broad Bellevue sidewalk, a perfect spot, the owners point out, for observing the daily parade of "cabbages and kings."

Sardella's, 30 Memorial Boulevard, next door to Puerini's (849-6312). Italian food, with more of a gourmet touch and slightly more formal atmosphere than its neighbor. Extensive menu of northern and southern specialties—Sogliole alla Fiorentina, Cotolette al Griglia. Excellent antipasti, including snail salad (a Rhode Island favorite) and fried mozzarella. Entrees from $10 to $22.

INEXPENSIVE

Salas' Dining Room, upstairs at 343 Thames, just around the corner from America's Cup Avenue. A true family dining room, popular with residents and visitors, Salas' supplies lots of noise, camaraderie, and good food at good prices. The restaurant's Guamanian owners offer Oriental as well as Italian spaghetti, sold by the pound or fraction thereof—lobster and clambakes, too. Dinner begins at 4 p.m. and the place fills quickly. No reservations are accepted, so come early or be prepared to wait. The adjoining bar, which serves excellent piña coladas, makes the wait easier.

International Café, 677 Thames, on Lower Thames Street (847-1033). Another favorite with locals, the International Café has a Philippine owner-chef, which makes for some tasty appetizers—lumpia, pancit behon—as well as more standard fare—shrimp scampi, scallops Parisienne, broiled scrod. Good food, reasonable prices (many dishes under $11) and an informal atmosphere. BYOB, but Fifth Ward Liquors is next door. No reservations. No credit cards, either.

Shore Dinner Hall, Waites Wharf, off lower Thames. It's surprising there aren't more low-cost seafood shacks in Newport, but here's one where you can get a one-pound lobster for $10 and fried clam, shrimp, or scallop dinners for under $10. Not a shack, but informal with seating at picnic tables and the west wall overlooking the harbor. Good place to take the kids. Free parking.

Amsterdam's, 509 Thames (847-0550). An informal New York-style restaurant that serves fish and pasta but mostly chicken from its rotisserie in a variety of forms. You can pay $15 to less than $10 for dinner. American Express only.

Dragon Express, 82 Broadway, across from City Hall (847-1686). Newport isn't known for its Chinese food, but Dragon Express, a small, informal shop several blocks from Washington Square, serves up familiar American-Oriental dishes at prices under $10.

Sportsman's Restaurant, 657 Park Avenue, Portsmouth (683-0039). Good seafood served in a casual, relaxed atmosphere at the north end of Aquidneck; popular with locals and Newporters who want to get away from town. Dining room open until 10; lunch specials served in early afternoon.

PUB FOOD AND SANDWICHES

Mudville's Restaurant, 8 Marlborough Street, near the Gateway Center. Mudville's serves light meals and daily specials, but its sandwiches, especially its cheeseburgers, are the real attraction. Because it's a sports bar too, there are plenty of televisions going, which is no surprise: it's owned by Kevin Stacom, a former Boston Celtic. (And the guy with the wild hair and mustache guarding him in one photo on the wall? None other than Pat Riley, before the hair slick.) On warm nights there's a small outdoor cage, or bullpen, where you can enjoy the open air and watch the baseball at adjacent Cardine's Field.

Yesterday's, 28 Washington Square. You'll find as many locals as tourists here enjoying the burgers, "Yesterday's nachos," salads, and daily specials. Full meals as well as regular dishes,

Dining in Newport

many with a Mexican flair. A good, centrally located place to have a casual meal. The adjoining wine bar—straight ahead as you enter—serves more imaginative dishes at slightly higher, but still reasonable, prices.

Brick Alley Pub, 140 Thames, around the corner from Washington Square. Another popular place, Brick Alley has its own "ultimate nacho" supporters and a menu strong on soups, sandwiches and salads. It began life in the 1970s as a German restaurant (under different owners) so there's a Biergarten out back where you can sit under the stars—or summer mist, as the case may be.

Griswold's Restaurant, 103 Bellevue Avenue, has front windows that roll up French café-style. Mexican food, sandwiches, and some seafood specials. Nice spot, away from the bustle of downtown.

Marina Pub, Goat Island. Sailors from the yachts docked nearby and Newporters who want the illusion of leaving town make up many of the patrons here. The Pub serves sandwiches along with soups and basic meals all day. Steak and seafood dinners after 5 p.m. Great view of Newport across the harbor.

CHEAP EATS

Handy Lunch, 462 Thames, an easy walk from downtown. When BOC (British Oxygen Corporation) round-the-world racer Mike Plant returned to Newport after 27,000 singlehanded miles at sea, he headed straight for Gary's Handy Lunch and a late breakfast of steak, eggs, and homefries. America's Cup sailors—hearty eaters all—once regularly began the day here. Nothing fancy about this lunch counter, one of the last in the city, but you can fill up on American chop suey or hamburg steaks for under $5.

Franklin Spa, corner of Spring and Franklin Streets. Part variety store, part milk bar, this is a favorite place for breakfast and light lunches (meat loaf, hot turkey sandwich) served until 2 p.m. Except for the Burger King on Thames Street, this is the cheapest spot to eat downtown.

Newport Creamery, several locations, including Long Wharf Mall, Bellevue Avenue (near Almac's), and West Main Road, Middletown. Popular soda fountains (Jackie Kennedy Onassis has been known to stop by) with a basic menu of soups, salads, and sandwiches, all done well at very reasonable prices.

8
NIGHTLIFE

🙞🙞🙞🙞

IN HIS BOOK *Blue Highways,* traveler William Least Heat Moon bemoans the homogenization of the Newport he knew as a sailor stationed at the local navy base in the early sixties. And it's true. This is no longer the funky, wild Navy town-seaport, crammed with back-alley bars (many off-limits), featuring nightly brawls and Shore Patrol wagons permanently on guard at Blood Alley, now the relatively sedate junction of Thames and Pelham Streets. Condos and timeshare units have replaced the waterfront dives, the sailors' bars and strip joints have given way to upscale cafés where, as Moon relates, people sip Day-Glo drinks and 21 year olds of all ages find something to chat about. But despite its newfound quaintness, Newport is a long way from being dull in the evening. The bars and lounges may have been dressed up, but they're still around in great numbers, albeit a bit more impersonal. Entertainment has smoothed out as well, with virtually every restaurant and lounge offering a version of "soft" rock or easy-listening jazz.

One of the best ways to find the nightly entertainment of your choice is simply to wander the downtown and wharf areas until you hear something you like. As always, the best show is in the streets. At its busiest, Newport is thronged with a lively mixture of tourists and yachtsmen, locals and millionaires. And don't be surprised to see a famous face—Christopher Reeve, Donald Sutherland, Walter Cronkite, and Ted Turner (all sailors as well as celebrities) have been recent visitors. Best of all, the streets and wharves are free. One caution: Appearances to the contrary, drinking on the street or public parks and beaches is illegal in Newport, as it is in most of Rhode Island. One exception is the private wharves, many of which have conveniently located outdoor bars.

Many of the larger hotels offer entertainment, especially on weekends. The type of entertainment varies as lounges vie for tourist dollars (comedy clubs began sprouting in the early 90s), but jazz is a standby at places like the Hotel Viking, The Mainstay, and Waverleys lounge at the Newport Harbor Hotel. For local listings, check the *Newport Daily News,* the *Providence Journal* Weekend section on Friday, and *Newport This Week,* a free weekly published on Thursdays and available around town.

LIVE MUSIC

Blue Pelican, 40 West Broadway (847-5675), a few blocks up from Marlborough Street. Blues, folk, rock—the music, and the audience changes nightly at the Pelican. One of the few real live-music houses in Newport, the Pelican books national, regional and local talent. Rock and roll and dancing most Fridays and Saturdays; occasional under-21 afternoon sessions. Bluesman Paul Geremiah, who lives in Newport, plays here regularly.

One Pelham East, corner of Thames and Pelham Streets, offers rock and roll and dancing nightly during the summer. Dress code isn't in the vocabulary here, and most nights the place is filled with a friendly, lively, occasionally rowdy crowd.

Surf's Up, 91 Long Wharf. As you might expect, this fluorescent bar attracts a young, lively set. Day-Glo shots and beer are what's consumed here. Juke box downstairs, live rock and reggae in upstairs room.

Dancing

The Daisy in the basement of the Clarke Cooke House on Bannister's Wharf is still queen of the Newport discos. Often called the Candy Store, The Daisy attracts visitors from around the world and is generally packed on summer nights. Expect a long wait if you're not inside by 10 or 11 p.m. on weekends. Combined with the other bars in the Candy Store complex, including the ultra-exclusive Sky Bar, this is the place to see and be seen in summer Newport. Mix of all ages. Cover.

The Newport Club, upstairs at One Pelham East on Thames Street, across from Bannister's Wharf; entrance around the corner on Pelham Street. Somewhat younger crowd than the Daisy in this smart disco that began life as a British-sponsored sailor hangout during the last America's Cup campaign. Cover.

Christie's, on the harbor at 351 Thames, offers "adult" rock in the bar, and a somewhat livelier band outside, playing for a younger audience. Both arenas likely to be packed on summer weekends. No cover.

Maximillian's, 108 Williams Street, just off Bellevue Avenue. Younger clientele in a disco that has been popular for more than a decade. Located upstairs from Sully's Pub. Cover.

Tickets, Marriott Hotel on Long Wharf. DJ playing Top 40 dance music Wednesday through Saturday in summer. The gimmick here is you don't pay cash, you purchase tickets to obtain drinks.

Raffles, 3 Farewell Street, between Washington Square and Marlborough Street. Gay or straight, you'll find some of the liveliest dancing in town at this hole-in-the-wall club a few steps from Broadway. Other clubs come and go; this one's been around for years.

THEATER

There's some surprisingly good theater in Newport, and not just of the summer theater variety. Venues (and cast) may change, but some troupes have been in business for 10 years or longer.

Tifobet (The Incredibly Far Off Broadway Ensemble Theatre) has been around since 1977, performing what director John Chatty calls "theatrical events" in settings ranging from bars and public parks to more conventional stages. Adaptations or original scripts, TIFOBET always has something interesting to offer. For information call 847-1996, or check local listings.

Trist (The Rhode Island Shakespeare Theatre). As the name implies, this group specializes in adaptions of the Bard's work, but also does other dramatic work. Excellent productions, good acting under the direction (usually) of Robert Colonna. For reservations or ticket information call 849-7892.

Newport Playhouse & Cabaret Restaurant (848-7529), 102 Connell Highway, near Newport Bridge. Popular comedies year-round Fridays and Saturdays at 8:30, Sunday at 7:30 (show times). Tickets for the play alone are $15. With dinner (all-you-can-eat buffet with fresh fish, roast beef, stir fry, and so on) is $29.95 per person.

MOVIES

Newport is not a big cinema town, but there are several theaters downtown showing first-run (or close to it) movies.

Jane Pickens Theatre (846-5252), 49 Touro Street, on Washington Square. One of the last of the big single-screen theaters in Rhode Island and a welcome alternative to boxy multiplexes. Named for a singing and stage star of the 1940s who summers in Newport, the Jane Pickens shows off-beat or first-run European films of consistently good quality. The man in the lobby, greeting patrons and asking how everyone liked the movie, is owner Joe Jarvis, who got his start in the movie business in 1936 as an usher at the age of 16.

Opera House (847-3456), 19 Touro Street, Washington Square. The old theater has been divided into three screens, but there's still more of a homey feeling than in the newer complexes. All first runs.

9
SHOPPING

FOR SOME YEARS NOW, Newport has meant tourists and tourists mean there are lots of places to spend vacation money. Each spring new shops spring up like May flowers, and while some have about the same lifespan, others have established their places in the city's commerce.

Most of the newer shops are concentrated in the revitalized downtown and wharf areas. Nearest the Gateway Center, Long Wharf Mall and Brick Market Place contain enough stores to occupy the dedicated browser for an hour or two. There are too many places to mention, but you'll find stores like Ley's Century Store at 1 Long Wharf Mall, the closest thing to a department store in downtown Newport (with some local-interest gifts), that has been in business since 1796. In Brick Market, there's the Book Bay bookstore, which is worth a visit, several small outdoor cafés for lunch, and the Chocolate Soldier, which features Godiva chocolates.

Farther along America's Cup Avenue, you come to Bowen's and Bannister's wharves, once the center of Newport's busy sea

Walkway between Bannister's and Bowen's wharves. An excellent shopping area.

trade, now filled with shops catering to visitors. Some of the more established shops are Mykonos, which specializes in Greek clothing and objects, Irish Imports, where you can get an Irish knit sweater or a Sherlock Holmes-style deerstalker cap, and the Spring Pottery studio and shop. Many shops here carry quality goods and many stay open late on summer evenings; it's a pleasant place to stroll even if you're not buying.

The retail boom has carried on down Thames Street to Wellington Avenue and beyond. Some of the better shops are listed elsewhere in the chapter. There are more stores along Spring Street, which runs parallel to Thames Street, most of them concentrated between Memorial Boulevard and Washington Square. Bellevue Avenue has more shopping in the Casino Block and for a block or two north. Aside from the Casino proper, there are ground-level stores in the adjoining Travers Block, a medieval-style, half-timber building immediately to the north, and in the Audrain Building (note the beautiful terra-cotta column details) building to the south. The following list of stores is not meant to be complete. Half the fun of shopping is discovering stores for yourself.

ART GALLERIES AND CRAFT SHOPS

William Vareika Fine Arts, 212 Bellevue Avenue (849-6149). One of the larger galleries in New England dealing with "museum quality" American art of the eighteenth, nineteenth, and early twentieth centuries. Vareika's specialty is work by artists who have some Newport connection, including paintings, drawings, and prints by such artists as John La Farge, John F. Kensett, Childe Hassam, and Edward M. Bannister. Open seven days in summer, Monday–Saturday from 10 a.m. to 6 p.m., Sunday from 1–6 p.m., or by appointment.

Roger King Fine Arts, 21 Bowen's Wharf (847-4359). Another fine arts dealer, buying and selling American and some European paintings from the eighteenth to twentiethth century. King only buys what he likes (and advises customers the same). Marine, scenics, but few portraits. King is an expert in early African-American artists. The gallery is on the second and third floors. Open daily 10 a.m.–6 p.m. or by appointment.

Spring Bull Studio, 1 Bull Street, at corner of Spring (849-9166). One portion of this relatively new gallery features a semi-permanent collection by area artists, the other presents shows that change monthly. Mostly representational, with lots of seascapes, including those by well-known local artist Richard Grosvenor (William F. Buckley collects him), and portraits.

Spring Bull is also a working studio, so it's likely some of the artists will be there and painting while you visit. Open Wednesday through Sunday from 12 noon to 5 p.m.

Deblois Gallery, 138 Bellevue (847-9977). Formed by an artists' cooperative, this small gallery also features local and area painters with regularly changing shows.

Arnold Art Gallery, 210 Thames (847-2273). An art supply store that has expanded into a gallery over the years. Regular shows of local and area artists, plus lots of old prints.

Hydrangea House Gallery, 16 Bellevue Avenue (846-4435). Original paintings and drawings, many from local artists. The two-room gallery offers a mix of representational and abstract work.

Viewpoint, 105 Swinburne Row, Brick Market Place (849-2328). Picture framing shop, but also lots of prints and posters of America's Cup boats and other subjects of local interest.

Fisher Gallery, 481 (Lower) Thames. Another framing shop, Fisher also sells paintings, prints, and engravings of local and regional (including the Southwest) interest.

ANTIQUES

Franklin Street, which runs between Thames and Spring streets beside the U.S. Post Office, is the closest thing to "antique row" in Newport. But there are many more shops, farther along Spring, on Bellevue Avenue, and interspersed around the city. There's some junk, some overpriced "collectibles" and nostalgia items, but there are also many fine—and costly—period pieces. You're not likely to uncover any steals—these dealers know their business—but you might find that Louis XIV desk or Ming vase you've been searching for. Although you'll find shops open most days during summer, many owners are notoriously casual about keeping regular hours, so it's either call ahead or catch-as-you-can.

John Gidley House, 22 Franklin Street (846-8303). Fine eighteenth- and nineteenth-century French furniture—no reproductions here—and many chandeliers and lamps.

A & A Gaines, 40 Franklin Street (849-6844). Specializes in eighteenth- and early nineteenth-century "top of the line" furnishings, clocks, China Trade items (porcelain, silver), and nautical antiques, including instruments and ship models.

Smith Marble Ltd., 44 Franklin Street (846-7689). Museum quality Rose Medallion and Rose Mandarin porcelain vases (actually Rose Canton, says owner Ada V. Smith) most from the 1800s; also French porcelain, china, crystal, and English and French furniture. This shop is on the corner of Franklin and Spring. There's an annex shop at 99 Spring. Open seven days from May to November.

The Drawing Room of Newport, 221 Spring Street, near Franklin (841-5060). The owners describe their wares as ninetheenth-century "decorative arts," European as well as American in origin. They specialize in items from Newport estates. Open 10:30 a.m.–5 p.m. Monday and Thursday–Saturday.

A. H. Bozyan Store, 140 Bellevue Avenue (847-0012). Edith Bozyan operates what she says is the oldest antique store in Newport on the site of her father's Oriental rug store which, in turn, was the oldest such store in the country. The shop consists of two long rectangular rooms filled with great clutter. You might find a treasure among her collection of rugs, furniture, china, and especially paintings. Edith taught painting in New York and elsewhere for many years, and she has amassed a good number of fine ones, ranging from huge pieces that once hung in Newport's great houses to smaller watercolors. She also has many antique frames. A woman of unusual intellect and character, Edith generally opens shop in the afternoon (not on Sundays), when she greets friend and stranger alike in the closest thing to a salon in Newport.

Shopping
SPECIALTY SHOPS

Full Swing, 474 Thames (849-9494). Vintage fabric and furniture shop that's gaining a national reputation. Articles in magazines such as *House & Garden* have helped, as have outlets in wholesale designer salons around the country. Writer Thomas McGuane has owner Michele Mancini's popular Yippee-ei-o cowboy fabric in his Montana bunkhouse. Bruce Springsteen has a swath or two of the Carmen Miranda floral print. Mancini lucked out several years ago when she found 16,000 yards of Barkcloth (sort of a craggy cotton weave) in a Virginia warehouse. She bought it and now reproduces the weave for draperies and for upholstering her 1930s, '40s and '50s era furniture. Fabrics—she'll mail a sample for $10—cost between $22 and $72 a yard. Yippee-ei-o cotton duck sells for $48 a yard.

Thames Glass, 688 (Lower) Thames (846-0576). Glassblower Matthew Buechner creates beautiful glass objects—vases, bowls, perfume bottles—in his shop adjacent to this retail showroom at the end of Thames Street. His work has been collected by the Corning Museum of Glass in Corning, New York (where his father served as president of Steuben Glass) and the Frauenau Museum of Glass in Germany, and has also been featured in the Smithsonian mail order catalog. Visitors can watch workers fire and blow glass at the shop, which Matthew and his wife Adrian opened in 1981. Anything that is even slightly flawed—something as minute as an iron spot from the blowpipe—is sold as a second at 50 percent off or more.

Cadeaux du Monde, 130 Bellevue Avenue, near Memorial Boulevard (848-0550). The owners of this eclectic shop that features clothes and art objects from 40 developing nations say their store is an "alternative trading organization"—they don't exploit Third World craftspeople, they work directly with them. The owners (one, Kate Dyer, was a Peace Corps volunteer) are happy to give you the story behind each of their sundry items. They have shirts from Guatemala, bangles from Zimbabwe, handwoven rugs from Pakistan and Afghanistan, statuary, and jewelry.

Rue de France, 78 Thames (846-3636) specializes in fine imported French lace curtains and has gained a national reputation through its catalog sales. Newport, where owner Pamela Kelley lives, is the only retail outlet. The store also sells the work of French artisans, from Provence specifically, including tableware, terra-cotta pots (some filled with flower-scented honey), and herbs and perfume. *Ouvert* 10:30–5:30 seven days in summer. The toll-free number for catalog orders is 800-7770998.

Third & Elm Press, 29 Third Street in the Point, is run by German natives Alexander and Ilse Buchert Nesbitt, who sell their own woodblock prints, Christmas cards, notepaper, and books. Much of the work in this homey shop features local scenes. Open Monday–Saturday 9 a.m. to 5 p.m.

Indesign at 10 Long Wharf Mall (847-4705) is a classy gift shop offering porcelain, crystal, original oils and prints, and sundry items large and small. All exhibit one trait, says owner Betty Teitz—good design. Name brands include Lalique, Limoges, Kosta Boda, and Baccarat.

Cabbages & Kings, 214 Bellevue Avenue, in the Casino Block. One of Newport's oldest shops, Cabbages & Kings, as the name indicates, sells a little bit of everything—fine porcelain, glassware, figurines, clocks, and even furniture. If the denizens of the Gilded Age were still around, this is one place they'd shop while in town.

Army and Navy Surplus, 262 Thames. This place, a Newport institution that has been written up in *Vogue* of all places, is an Army/Navy store gone wild. Besides the usual pea coats, Navy shoes and Marine knives, you can buy diving helmets, trenching tools, field radios, and regular camping equipment. Part museum, part antique store, you can spend an hour browsing its cluttered aisles. You can also shop for regular Levis, flannel shirts, and some of the cheapest "Newport" T-shirts in town.

Carroll Michael & Co. Pharmacy, 115 Bellevue Avenue (849-4488). To call this a drugstore would be misleading. There is a registered pharmacist behind the counter, but the store itself is a mix of apothecary, perfumery, and gourmet pantry. There's potpourri, travel kit items, English preserves, and top lines of cosmetics—all in a reproduced colonial setting.

Ebenezer Flagg, 65 Touro Street, on the corner of Spring (846-1891) makes customized flags and pennants, but also sells many stock historical and national flags, as well as boat ensigns and windsocks. Ebenezer Flagg was a patriot who died during the Revolution. Company founder Leo Waring, who set the store near the (now underground) spring around which the town was built, found Flagg's name on a headstone in the Common Burial Ground, and named the store in his honor. Leo, who died in the late 1980s, was a Massachusetts native who believed Newport was one of the last true bastions of democracy in the world.

Vinland Wine Cellars, Eastgate Shopping Center, 909 East Main Road, Middletown (848-5161). Retired Navy captain Richard Alexander began planting his vineyards in 1977; several years later he began selling his first vintages at this store in Middletown. Visitors can sample his Vidal blanc, Seyval blanc, Viking red, and other varieties and also tour the winery to see how and where the wine is made. Open daily 10 a.m.–5p.m., noon to 5 p.m. on Sundays. (Vinland, like Sakonnet Vineyards in Little Compton, can sell wine on Sundays because it falls under the category of "farm produce.") Next door at Eastgate is the CHOCOLATE MASTER candy shop, selling many varieties of hand-dipped chocolate and truffle concoctions.

CLOTHING

There's nothing that could be called a Newport "look" in the sense that there is a London look or a California look. Newporters tend to dress for the weather, as lightly as feasible in the summer, as warmly as possible during the damp, blowy winters when many of the women resort to long johns. The clothing tends to be practical, casual and fairly nondescript. If anything, Newporters don't pay much attention to clothes and rarely dress up—unless it's black tie for a ball—preferring blue blazers and slacks or skirts to three-piece suits and the equivalent. One exception is clothing you wear on or around the sea—foul weather gear and accessories. Here are some stores worth a visit.

Team One, 547 Thames Street (847-2368). Sea Gear, Henri Lloyd, and other excellent lines of sea-going clothing suited for onshore, offshore or just near-the-shore wear.

J.T.'s Ship Chandlery, 364 Thames Street (846-7256) also carries foul-weather clothing and light and heavy cotton and wool sweaters.

Explorer's Club, 140 Spring Street (846-8465). Real outdoorswear in natural fabrics, including waxed cotton "oilskins" from Scotland, heavy wool shirts from C. C. Filson of Seattle (which outfitted prospectors during the Klondike Gold Rush) and Barbour of Great Britain. Because natural fabrics must be kept up, the store also sells Driza-Bone and Barbour Thornproof dressings, from Australia and England respectively.

Island Windsurfing, 86 Aquidneck Avenue, Middletown (846-4421), at the foot of Memorial Boulevard. Bathing suits, surfing fashions and other active wear at this popular water sports shop.

Ley's Century Store, 1 Long Wharf Mall, advertises that it has been in business since 1796, making it one of the oldest family-owned department stores in the United States. Complete line of straightforward, even conservative, clothing for men, women, and children. This is the place to get those Brenton red pants to fit in with summering New York Yacht Club members.

Potter & Co., 172 Thames. Started in 1907, this store is a favorite with locals and offers the real Newport look—Levi cords and lots of Woolrich.

Shopping

Lily's of the Alley, 64 Spring Street, near corner of Touro Street (846-7545). Specializes in off-price cotton women's clothing (Indian imports), tapestries, bedspreads and its own line of "essential" oils. Very popular with locals.

Potjandozie of Newport (849-1644). Owner Rachel Balaban doesn't have her own retail store yet for the innovative line of "expandable" clothing she's developed for children, but you can find them at the Spring Street Collection, 134 Spring Street (near Trinity Church). Balaban's brightly colored, hand-sewn overalls (reversible for fall) have ties at the shoulders and roll-up cuffs so they fit from age eight months to three years. Potjandozie (the word means "gosh" or "golly" in Dutch) clothes include dresses, shorts, and hats and can also be bought through the Hand in Hand catalog (1-800-543-4343).

BOOKSTORES

Corner Book Shop, 418 Spring Street (846-8406). Larry Whitford presides over a strong collection of rare and first edition books, many with beautiful graphics. Also plenty of used paperbacks, including early potboilers, and vintage postcards. This is the place to look for a hard-to-find volume. And if it's not too busy, the proprietor will take you on in chess or cribbage. Open daily except Sundays, 1–5 p.m. and 6:30–9 p.m.

Waldenbooks, Bellevue Shopping Center (near Almacs) and Newport Mall on Connell Highway. Popular chain with the latest in fiction and nonfiction. Both locations have excellent sections on books of local and regional interest.

Anchor & Dolphin Books, at 30 Franklin Street, across from the post office (846-6890). As much an antique store as a bookseller, Anchor & Dolphin owners James Hinck and Ann Marie Wall are experts in rare books. Many fields, especially art, architecture, gardening and antiquarian material. Open irregularly, but most afternoons.

The Book Bay, Brick Market Place (846-3033). Maybe the best all-around bookstore in Newport for browsing. Paperbound classics and bestsellers in hardcover. Sections on local interest, sailing, and children's books. *New York Times Book Review* on sale.

Armchair Sailor Bookstore, 543 Thames (847-4252). Many books of marine interest, including new releases and older first editions. Boating magazines from around the world. Also a selection of interesting Penguin-type classic literature. Another good place for browsing—the owners even provide a coffee area overlooking the harbor. Parking behind the store on Lower Thames.

10
IF YOU COME BY SEA
41° 29' N, 71° 19' W

🌊🌊🌊🌊

OF ALL THE WAYS to approach Newport, the most memorable is by sea. When you turn into the harbor after passing through the East Passage of Narragansett Bay between the southern neck of Aquidneck and Conanicut Island, Newport unfolds before you like a miniature colonial city. The most obvious landmark for the sailor is the tall white steeple of Trinity Church. The white is reflected in the hundreds of white hulls bobbing at moorings the length of the harbor.

GETTING HERE

First, of course, you'll have to find your way to the entrance of Narragansett Bay, which can be a problem, especially with the occasional thick summer fog. The chart for Newport and Narragansett Bay is 13221. For a smaller-scale look at Newport

Harbor, you can use U.S. Coast Guard Chart 13223, although it's not absolutely needed. There is heavy commercial traffic steaming in and out of Narragansett Bay; recommended approach charts from the west and east are 12300 and 13218.

The bay entrance is marked by Brenton Tower, 1.5 miles out. The Texas tower structure shows a light (group flash, every 10 seconds) from a height of 87 feet, and has a powerful fog horn and a RDF beacon with a range of 10 miles. Also visible should be the Point Judith Light, six miles to the southwest, flashing every 15 seconds, and, 1.4 miles NNW, the Beavertail Light at the southern tip of Conanicut, flashing green every 5 seconds. Make absolutely sure the lights are properly identified before proceeding. Once past Brenton Tower, boats only have to keep clear of the Brenton Reef shoal area to the northeast, close to Newport Neck.

Once inside the East Passage, the going is easy. James Fenimore Cooper, writing in *The Red Rover,* described Newport as one of America's most important ports at one time, "Enjoying the four great requisites of a safe and commodius haven—a placid basin, an outer harbor, and a convenient roadstead with a clear offing."

In summer, you'll find Newport Harbor crowded with pleasure boats of all sizes and vintage, from classic sailing schooners to tiny catboats to slick racing machines, interspersed with commercial fishing vessels and barges. This is nothing new for Newport. More than two hundred years ago, the city was homeport for a good two hundred ships engaged in foreign trade and another three to four hundred coastal traders.

There are a number of areas affording safe anchorage between Newport and Conanicut (Jamestown), but the harbor proper is generally understood to extend from the farthest indentation of Brenton Cove on the south to the Newport Bridge on the north. Except for smaller powerboats, those wishing to enter the northern section of the harbor must detour around Goat Island because of the causeway (vertical clearance, 14

If You Come by Sea

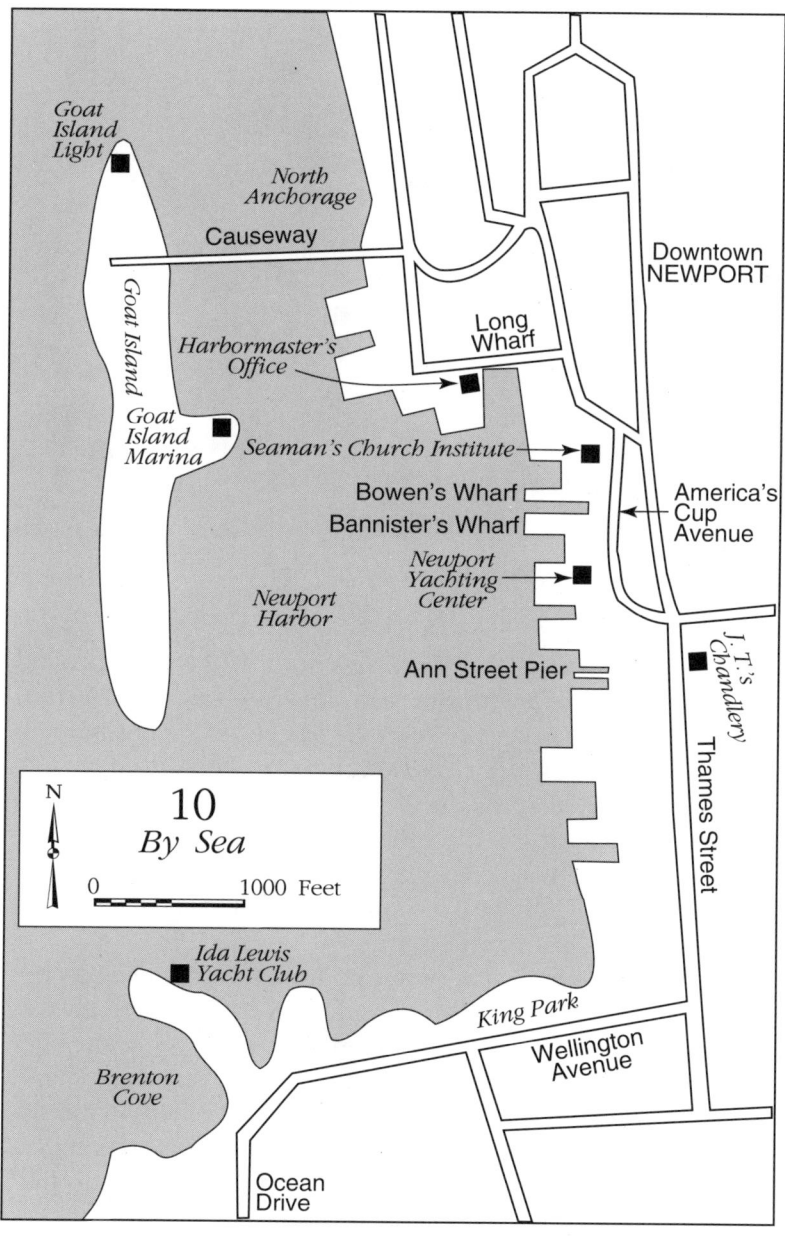

10
By Sea

Heading for the mark in the Newport Regatta.

feet) that links the island with Newport. The two approved harbor anchorages are in Brenton Cove, in the southwestern extension of the harbor, between the Ida Lewis Yacht Club and Little Ida Lewis Rock. Overnight stops, or emergency anchorings, are okay north of the Goat Island causeway. A quarantine area for international travelers has been set aside north of the causeway, off the east bank of Goat Island. To be certain, check in with the harbormaster, either at 847-4370 or on Channel 16 on your marine radio.

Newport Harbor is well protected from the prevailing southwest wind, which generally begins the day as a light northwesterly. In the fall, when cold fronts from Canada bring stronger northerly winds, the water in Brenton Cove kicks up a bit and it's best to move north to calmer waters in the lee of Goat Island. Whatever the season, you'll find Newport has a centuries-old tradition of catering to seafarers, and you are likely to find whatever services you or your boat require.

If You Come by Sea

MOORINGS AND DOCKAGE

In the busy season, finding a mooring will be your first and hardest task. Here is a list of the major firms providing dockage, moorings, repairs, and other services.

Oldport Marine Services, Sayer's Wharf, beside the Mooring Restaurant (847-9109). Oldport rents moorings throughout the main harbor for $28/night for boats up to 40 feet, $33/night for larger boats. Reserve ahead or call Oldport on Channel 16. Most of the moorings are within easy rowing distance of shore, or you can take advantage of Oldport's launch service: $1.25 per person each way in the main harbor, $1.50 per person to the farther reaches of Brenton Cove or the Point. Runs from 7 a.m. to 1 a.m. at the height of the season.

Newport Mooring Service, 4 Wheatland Court, Newport 02840. (846-7535). Neill Gray has about eight moorings available for visiting boats, located near the southern portion of the harbor, east of Ida Lewis Yacht Club and off King Park. A little removed from the center of town, but a quieter spot to enjoy a sunset. Charge is $25/night, and Gray suggests calling or writing ahead.

Newport Yachting Center, Commercial Wharf in the heart of the harbor (849-4703 or 847-9047). The Yachting Center stores boats in the winter, but changes to a multipurpose site for boat shows, rendezvous, and fairs in warmer months. Just the same, there's often space at the dock at $2/foot per night, as well as a fuel dock.

Goat Island Marina, at the southeast end of Goat Island (849-5655 or 849-2600), is somewhat removed from the city (which can be a blessing), but still a well-equipped facility that serves as home to many of the transatlantic sailors who come to Newport. Can handle boats from 20 to 120 feet. Charge $2.10/foot. The marina has the harbor's only marine head pumpout station. Other shoreside amenities include showers, a laundromat and restaurant-pub. It was in the Marina

Pub some years ago that several sailors, after a few pints, dreamed up the idea for a singlehanded round-the-world race, which now begins, and ends, in Newport every four years. On the second floor of the marina office is the headquarters for the United States Yacht Racing Union. Also available nearby is a repair shop for gasoline and diesel marine engines, a small variety store, liquor store, and an Avis car rental office (846-1843).

Bannister's, at the end of Bannister's Wharf (846-4500) may not be the largest marina in town, but they've catered to some famous boats—Ted Turner's *Courageous* was based here during its successful 1977 defense of the America's Cup. Tying up here also puts you in the thick of Newport's nightlife and close to several of its best restaurants. Overnight charge is $2 a foot; fuel dock and full hookups. Guest rooms also available, above the marina and farther up the wharf.

Boats tied up between Bowen's and Bannister's wharves in the heart of the waterfront district.

Christie's Marina, off 351 Thames Street (847-3918 or 847-5400). Also monitors Channel 16. Room for about 50 transients at this popular dock behind Christie's Restaurant. Electricity, water, showers. Dockage fees "fluctuate," according to dockmaster, but you shouldn't pay more than $2/foot.

Newport Harbor Hotel and Marina (formerly the Treadway Inn), just north of Bannister's and Bowen's Wharves (847-9000, ext. 757). Mostly reserved for transients at $2/ft. per night. Call ahead or on Channel 16.

Newport Yacht Club, Long Wharf (846-9410). Reciprocal privileges for other club members, including dock space when available, usually during the week. Call on Channel 9.

Ida Lewis Yacht Club, at the south end of the main harbor, offers reciprocal privileges to fellow yacht club members, including overnight moorings. Cost $30. Call 849-1969 or call on

Boats tied up at Bowen's Wharf.

Channel 9. Ida Lewis, for whom the club is named, was a Newport lightkeeper, who began her auspicious career as heroine in 1854 at the age of 12, when she rescued four persons from the stormy bay waters near the site of the present club. She saved many more during her life (she died in 1911) and in 1881 was awarded a Congressional medal for heroism.

City Facilities (Dinghy tie-ups). The city provides several places where dinghies can be tied up. One is the Ann Street Pier, just south of Christie's Restaurant, in the heart of the harbor. A private contractor runs the tie-up, on rafts near the end of a long pier topped with a Victorian cupola, and charges a modest fee, about $1/hour. An attendant keeps an eye on things. For those at the south end of the harbor, the city operates the Stone Pier, just east of the Ida Lewis dock, where tie-ups are free. Private Bowen's Wharf, one wharf north of Bannister's, permits stops for reasonable amounts of time. Also, there are several informal landing spots, including a series of driftways that lead up from the north side of the harbor in the Point section. Best to bring a lock and not block access.

Out-of-Town Tie-Ups

Conancut Marina, East Ferry, Jamestown (423-1556), across the East Passage on Conanicut Island. Although removed from Newport, the marina is in the heart of downtown Jamestown, a pleasant place with a quieter (but still resort-like) pace than Newport. Everything you'll need is within easy walking distance. Rental moorings at $30 a night, which includes launch service. Dockmaster monitors Channel 71.

Little Harbor Marina, west shore of Aquidneck in Portsmouth (683-5700). Somewhat distant from Newport proper (c. 7 nautical miles, 15 minutes by car), Little Harbor (also known as Ted Hood's yard) is a full-service marina with the capability to do major repairs. This is the commissioning site for Hood's Little Harbor cruising yachts, and some of the best

If You Come by Sea 159

yardmen in the business will be found here. Dockage fee is $1.25/ft. per night, and reservations are "recommended."

East Passage Yachting Center, just north of Little Harbor (683-4000). Another full-service center with every conceivable marine-related business on the premises. Also a restaurant and well-stocked chandlery. Capable of handling yachts up to 60 feet—for longer boats advance notice is advisable. Charge: $1.80/ft. per night.

ESPECIALLY FOR SAIL

Shore Sail Company, 7 Merton Road, Newport (849-7997). The sailmakers at Shore's home loft are experienced—and champion—racers and sailors. They're also unfailingly easy to work with. Pickup and delivery. New sails, repairs, and gear.

Jasper & Bailey Sailmakers, 64 Halsey Street, in the north end of the city (847-8796). Racing and cruising sails, modern and traditional. Washing and repairing. Ask for Aaron Jasper.

J. T.'s Chandlery, 364 Thames Street (846-7256), downtown Newport. Close to the waterfront, J. T.'s has been in the marine hardware business since 1909. As much a boutique as a chandlery, the store sells varnish and Vaurnet sunglasses, shackles and fishermen's sweaters.

Jamestown Distributors, 28 Narragansett Avenue, Jamestown (423-2520). If J. T.'s doesn't have it, try here. Full stock of equipment and gear—the company supplies many builders. For a free catalog, write them at P.O. Box 348, Jamestown, RI 02835.

Team One, 547 Thames Street (847-2368). Outdoor wear of all kinds. Proprietor Martha Parker is an accomplished sailor who's tested what she sells.

Armchair Sailor Bookstore, 543 Thames Street, near Wellington Avenue (847-4252). Not only a great bookstore to browse or buy in, with new and rare old books of all kinds, but the place to go if you have a navigational question. Complete charts and sailing instructions for distant ports. Owner Ron Barr is an experienced offshore sailor and navigator. To order charts call 1-800-292-4278.

Ebenezer Flagg, 65 Touro Street (846-1891). Yachting ensigns and international flags. Also available at FLYING COLORS, 468 Thames (846-0418).

SUNDRY SERVICES AND SUPPLIES

Seaman's Church Institute, 18 Market Square, off America's Cup Avenue, just north of Bowen's Wharf. The institute, built by Bellevue Avenue benefactors, has been an all-around haven for seafarers since 1919, providing showers, public restrooms, a limited number of cheap rooms, and a lunch counter serving modestly priced breakfast and lunch. There's a sitting room and small library where you can take a breather. Upstairs is the Chapel of the Sea. Open seven days a week. Call 847-4260.

Engine Repair—Murphy Marine, Goat Island (849-2010), and Oldport Marine Services on Sayer's Wharf (847-9109) for diesel repairs, especially.

Food and Groceries—The Corner Store & Deli, 372 Thames, is within easy walking distance of the waterfront and provides basic food and grocery supplies.

The nearest supermarkets are Almacs on Bellevue Avenue, just around the corner from Memorial Boulevard, and A&P in the Bellevue Shopping Center, both accustomed to provisioning yachts.

APPENDIX
Services, Emergencies and Helpful Phone Numbers

TOURIST INFORMATION

Gateway Center (Newport County Convention & Visitors Bureau), 23 America's Cup Avenue (401-849-8098; toll-free, 1-800-326-6030). The main source of tourist-related information in the area.

Newport County Chamber of Commerce, 45 Valley Road, Middletown (401-847-1600).

AAA, 700 Aquidneck Avenue (corner of Green End Avenue), Middletown (401-847-6384).

Tourist Promotion Division, Rhode Island Department of Economic Development, has a toll-free information service for out-of-state calls, 1-800-556-2484.

HEALTH SERVICES

Newport Hospital, corner of Broadway and Friendship Street (846-6400).

Newport County Medical Treatment Office, 67 Valley Road, Middletown (847-4950). Private clinic for minor medical emergencies and health problems. Open 8 a.m.–8 p.m. Monday to Friday, and 9 a.m.–5 p.m. Saturdays and Sundays.

Naval Regional Medical Center, Third Street, Newport (841-3771). Provides emergency service for retired or active military personnel and their families. Open 7:30 a.m.–10 p.m. weekdays, 10 a.m.–10 p.m. Saturdays and Sundays.

EMERGENCY NUMBERS

Dial 911 for police and medical emergencies.

Newport Police, 120 Broadway (847-1212).

Middletown Police, 9 Berkeley Avenue (846-1104).

LIBRARY

Newport has one public library on Spring Street in Aquidneck Park, one-half block from Memorial Boulevard (847-8720). THE NEWPORT ROOM has many volumes on area history and architecture. Good selection of Sunday newspapers from around the country. Open Mondays 1–9 p.m., Tuesday to Thursday 9:30 a.m.–9 p.m., Fridays and Saturdays 9:30 a.m.–6 p.m.

Appendix

POST OFFICES

The main post office is in the Federal Building on Thames at the corner of Memorial Boulevard. Windows open Monday through Friday from 8:30 a.m.–5 p.m. and Saturdays 8:30 a.m.–12 noon. A satellite post office, open weekdays, is located at 195 Broadway, just south of Newport Hospital.

INDEX

A. H. Bozyan Store, 144
A. P. White Store, 101
A & A Gaines, 144
Abraham Brown House, 99
Abraham Rodriguez Rivera
  House, 76
Accommodations, 110-21
Admiral Benbow Inn, 118
Admiral Farragut Inn, 118
Admiral Fitzroy Inn, 114
Ailman House, 80
Airport, 17
Air tours, 58
Alexander Jack Jr. House, 82
Almy House, 86-87
Amsterdam's, 132
Anchorages, 152, 154

Anchor & Dolphin Books, 149
Andrew's Restaurant, 129
Anna's Victorian Connection,
  113
Antiques, 143-44
Architecture
  mansions, 25-26
  Victorian houses, 92-97
Armchair Sailor Bookstore, 150,
  159-60
Army and Navy Surplus, 146
Arnold Art Gallery, 143
Art, Newport Art Museum, 50
Art galleries, 142-43
Astor, Caroline, 32
Augustus Lucas House, 80
Automobiles, 20

Bailey's Beach, 65-66
Bannister House, 81-82
Bannister's, 156
Bannister's Wharf, 118
Barker House, 76-77
Barton, Col. William, 60
Baseball, 72-73
Battleship Cove, 105
Beaches, 63-66
Beattie House, 82
Beavertail Light, 108-9
Bed-and-breakfasts, 112-18
Bed & Breakfast Newport, 113
Bed & Breakfast of Rhode Island, 113
Beechwood, 32-33
Belcourt Castle, 35
Bell House, 77
Belmont, Oliver Hazard Terry, 35
Benjamin Howland House, 88
Bennett House, 87
Benson, John Howard, 87
Beriah Brown House, 82
Berkeley, Dean George, 58-59, 60
Best Western Mainstay Inn, 119
Bicycles, 21
Billings-Coggeshall House, 82
Billy Bottomore House, 81
Birds, Norman Bird Sanctuary, 60
Black Pearl, 124-25
Black Regiment Memorial, 63
Black Ships Festival, 67
Block Island, ferry to, 21
Blue Pelican, 136
Boating, 151-60
Boat shows, 69
The Book Bay, 150

Bookstores, 149-50
Borden, Lizzie, 103-4, 105
Bottomore House, 81
Bours House, 82
Bouvier, Jacqueline, 51-52, 53
The Breakers, 29
Breakers Stable/Carriage House, 29-30
Brenton Counting House, 91
Brick Alley Pub, 133
Brick Market, 76
Brinley Victorian Inn, 117
Brown (Abraham) House, 99
Brown (Beriah) House, 82
Bubbling Rock, 45
Budget Motor Inn, 119
Buses, 20-21
Business district, 19

Cabbages & Kings, 146
Cadeaux du Monde, 145-46
Caleb Claggett House, 89
Campbell House, 89
Campgrounds, 120-21
Candy, Capt. Henry, 49-50
Captain John Warren House, 91
Captain Kidd, 13, 109
Captain Peter Simon House, 89
Captain Robert Gray House, 99
Captain William Read House, 87
Card House, 81
Carr House, 79-80
Carroll Michael & Co. Pharmacy, 147
Cars, 20
Channing, William Ellery, statue of, 56

Channing Memorial Church,
  53-54
Chart House Restaurant, 130
Chase-Cory House, 101-2
Chateau-Sur-Mer, 28
Christie's, 128, 137
Christie's Marina, 157
Christopher Townsend House
  and Studio, 90
Churches, 40-41, 53-55, 63
Cinema, 138-39
Claggett, William, 89
Claggett (Caleb) House, 89
Claggett (William) House, 88-89
Clarendon Court, 44
Clarke Cooke House, 125-26
Clarke (Sherman) House, 90
Clarke Street Meeting House,
  77-78
Classic Yacht Regatta, 69
Clement C. Moore House, 94
Cliffside Inn, 115
Cliff Walk, 45-46
Clothing
  shops for, 147-49
  for touring, 15-16
Coddington House, 86
Coleman House, 96
Colonel George Waring House,
  95
Colonial buildings, 36-43, 46,
  74-75
Colonial period, 12-13
Colony House, 36-37
Commodore Edgar House, 96
Common Burying Ground, 88
Conanicut, 106-9
Conanicut Marina, 158

Cooper, James Fennimore, 152
Corne, Michel Felice, 81
Corne House, 81
Cornell House, 79
Corner Book Shop, 149
Corporate Air Newport, 58
Cotton House, 83
Covell House, 91
Cozzens House, 88
Craft shops, 142-43
Crossways, 45

Daisy, The, 137
Dancing, 137-38
Daniel Carr House, 79-80
Dave & Eddie's, 129-30
Day trips, 98-109
Deblois Gallery, 143
de Ternay, Admiral d'Arsac, 40,
  42
Dining, 122-34
Dockage and moorings, 155-59
Dr. Cotton House, 83
Doubletree Inn, 111-12
Douglas Campbell House, 89
Dragon Express, 132
The Drawing Room of Newport,
  144
Dress habits, for touring, 15-16
Driving to Newport, 16-17

Easton's Beach, 64
East Passage Yachting Center,
  159
Ebenezer Flagg, 147, 160
Ebenezer Hathaway House, 87

Edgar House, 96
Elisha Gibbs House, 79
Ellery House, 79
The Elms, 27-28
Emergency numbers, 162
Engine repair, 160
Entertainment, 135-39
Erastus Pease House, 83
Events, 66-69
Explorer's Club, 148
Ezra Stiles House, 78-79

Fall River, 103-6
Fall River Historical Society, 105
Festivals, 66-67
Films, 138-39
Finnegan's Inn at Shadow Lawn, 117
Fish, Mrs. Stuyvesant, 45
Fisher Gallery, 143
Fishing, 72
Flag Quarters, 118
Flying to Newport, 17
Folk festival, 67
Fort Adams, 52-53
Fort Adams State Park, 65
Fort Barton, 99
Fort Getty Recreation Area, 120
Fort Wetherill, 109
Francis Malbone House, 113-14
Franklin Spa, 133-34
Full Swing, 145

Gale House, 79
Gardens
Green Animals, 62
secret gardens tour, 66

Gardner (James) House, 89
Gardner Townsend House, 89
Gateway Center, 17-18
Geography, 16
George Topham House, 91
Gibbs House, 79, 82
Gideon Cornell House, 79
Gilded Age, 24-26
Goat Island Marina, 155-56
Goddard House, 81
Golf, 70
    PGA Seniors, 67-68
Gooseberry Beach, 65
Gray, Capt. Robert, 99
Gray House, 99
Green Animals, 62
Griswold's Restaurant, 133
Groceries, 160

Hammersmith Farm, 51-52
Handy Lunch, 133
Harbor, 151-60
Harbor Boat & Breakfast, 113
Harbor tours, 57-58
Hathaway House, 87
Health services, 162
Helicopter tours, 58
Hessian Hole, 63
Historic Hill and Washington Square, walking tour, 75-83
History, 12-14, 23
    historic buildings, 36-43, 46, 74-75
Honeyman Hall, 82-83
Hopkins, Dr. Samuel, 80
Hotels, 111-12
Hotel Viking, 112
Houses, on walking tours, 74-97

Index

Howard Johnson Lodge, 119
Howland House, 88
Hunt, Richard Morris, 25-26, 28, 33
Hunter House, 41-43, 91
Hydrangea House, 117
Hydrangea House Gallery, 143

Ice cream, 101
Ida Lewis Yacht Club, 157-58
Indesign, 146
Inn at Castle Hill, 116
Inns, 112-18
International Café, 131
International Tennis Hall of Fame, 48-50
Island Cemetery, 88
Island Windsurfing, 148
Ivy Lodge, 114-15

Jack House, 82
Jai alai, 73
Jailhouse Inn, 115
James, Henry, 24, 25
James Gardner House, 89
James House, 91
Jamestown, 106-9
Jamestown Distributors, 159
Jamestown Fire Memorial, 108
Jamestown Museum, 108
Jamestown Windmill, 108
Jane Pickens Theatre, 138-39
Jasper & Bailey Sailmakers, 159
Jazz festival, 67
Jeremiah Lawton House, 87
Jewish settlers, 37
Job Bennett House, 87

Job (John) Townsend House, 90
John Bannister House, 81-82
John Gidley House, 144
John Langley House, 83
John Pain House, 89-90
John Stevens House, 87
John Stevens Shop, 87
Johnston, Augustus, 80
Jonathan Almy House, 86-87
Jonathan Gibbs House, 82
Jonathan James House, 91
Joseph and Robert Rogers House, 76
Joseph Beattie House, 82
Joseph Stevens House, 88
Journey's End Motels, 119
J.T.'s Chandlery, 148, 159

Katherine Prescott Wormeley House, 95
Kennedy, Pres. John F., 51, 52, 53
Kidd, Capt., 13, 109
King Park, 65
Kingscote, 26-27

La Farge, John, 96
La Forge Casino, 130-31
La Forge Cottages, 114
Langley House, 83
La Petite Auberge, 126-27
Lawton House, 87
Le Bistro, 127
Levi Gale House, 79
Ley's Century Store, 148
Liberty Tree, 88
Libraries, 162

Newport Historical Society, 48
Redwood Library, 46
Lighthouse, Beavertail Light, 108-9
Lily's of the Alley, 149
Little Compton, 102-3
Little Harbor Marina, 158-59
Lizzie Borden House, 103-4
Lobster, 122, 123
Lucas House, 80

Mansions, 24-35
Marble House, 33, 35
Marina Pub, 133
Marinas, 155-59
Marine Museum at Fall River, 105
Marriott hotel, 111
Martha Pitman House, 90
Mason, George Champlin, 96
Maximillian's, 137
McKim, Charles, 95
Meadowlark Trailer Park, 120
Melville Ponds Campground, 120
Michel Felice Corne House, 81
Military displays
Battleship Cove, 105
Naval War College Museum, 53
Newport Artillery Company, 50
Miller Lite Hall of Fame tennis tournament, 68
Mill Street Inn, 116
Miramar, 44
Moore House, 94
The Mooring, 129
Moorings and Dockage, 155-59
Motels and motor lodges, 119-20
Movies, 138-39
Mudville's Restaurant, 132

Muriel's, 130
Museum of Yachting, 52-53
Museums, 47-53, 105, 108
Music, 136-37
Music festivals, 66-67

Narragansett Bay, 151-52
Nassau Hastie House, 80
Nature, 23-24
Cliff Walk and Ocean Drive, 43-46
Naval War College Museum, 53
Neighborhoods, 19
Newport
  contemporary profile, 14-15
  diversity of, 11-12
Newport Artillery Company, 50, 78
Newport Art Museum, 50
The Newport Club, 137
Newport Congregational Church, 54
Newport Courtyard, 119
Newport Creamery, 134
Newport Harbor, 151-60
Newport Harbor Hotel & Marina, 111, 157
Newport Harbor Tours, 58
Newport Helicopters Inc., 58
Newport Historical Society, 47-48
Newport Jazz and Folk Festivals, 67
Newport Marriott, 111
Newport Mooring Service, 155
Newport Music Festival, 66-67
Newport Playhouse & Cabaret Restaurant, 138
Newport Yacht Club, 157

Index

Newport Yachting Center, 155
Nichols, Jonathan, 42
Nightlife, 135-39
Norman Bird Sanctuary, 60
Norton Wilbour House, 81

Ocean Drive, 43-45
Ochre Court, 30-31
Oelrichs, Mrs. Herman ("Tessie"), 31
Old Colony & Newport Railway, 58
Old Nat's House, 90
Oldport Marine, 57
Oldport Maritime Services, 155
Old Stone Mill, 39
Onassis, Jacqueline Kennedy, 51-52, 53
One Pelham East, 136
Opera House, 139
Orientation, 17-18

Pain House, 89-90
Paradise Mobile Home Park, 120
Pease House, 83
Peckham House, 87
Peleg Barker House, 76-77
Perry House, 76
Perry Monument, 55
Peter Buliod (Perry) House, 76
PGA Seniors Golf, 67
The Pier, 128
Piracy, in Colonial period, 13
Pitman House, 90
Pitt's Head Tavern, 90-91
The Point, 83, 85
    walking tour, 83-92
Portsmouth Abbey, 63

Post offices, 163
Potjandozie of Newport, 149
Potter & Co., 148
Pratt House, 92, 94
Prescott, Gen. William, 60
Prescott Farm, 60-61
Preservation Society of Newport County, 25, 26
Puerini's, 130
Purgatory Chasm, 60

Quaker Meeting House, 54-55, 85
Quaker (Tom) Robinson House, 91
Queen Anne Inn, 118

Raffles, 137-38
Railway tours, 58
Read House, 87
Redwood Library, 46
Rhoades-Pease House, 78
Rhode Island House, 116
The Rhumb Line, 130
Richardson Peckham House, 87
Rivera House, 76
Robert Stevens House, 78
Robinson, Hannah, 89
Robinson House, 91
Rochambeau, Compte de, 78
    statue of, 57
Roger King Fine Arts, 142
Rogers House, 76
Rosecliff, 31-32
Rough Point, 44-45
Royal Plaza, 119
Rue de France, 146

Sabbatarian Meeting House, 47-48
Sachuest Beach, 64
Sailing, 71, 159-60
St. Mary's Church, 53
St. Paul's Methodist Church, 86
Sakonnet and Tiverton, 99-103
Sakonnet Vineyards, 102
Salas' Dining Room, 131
Samual Bours House, 82
Samuel Coleman House, 96
Samuel Pratt House, 92, 94
Samuel Tilton House, 97
Samuel Whitehorne House, 51
Sandy Point Beach, 66
Sanford Covell House, 91, 115-16
Sardella's, 131
Scales & Shells, 129
Sea approach, 151-52
Sea Fare Inn, 128
Seaman's Church Institute, 160
Seasons, for touring, 15
Sea View Motel, 120
Second Beach Family Campground, 120
Secret Gardens Tour, 66
Sherman Clarke House, 90
Shopping, 140-50
Shore Dinner Hall, 131-32
Shore Sail Company, 159
Sightsailing of Newport, 58
Sightseeing
   area attractions, 58-63
   beaches, 63-66
   churches, 40-41, 53-55, 63
   historic buildings, 36-43, 46
   mansions, 23-35
   museums, 47-53
   organized tours, 57-58
   special events, 66-69
   statues, 55-57
Simon House, 89
Sindney L. Wright Museum, 108
Skinner House, 95
Smith Marble Ltd., 144
Smuggling, in Colonial period, 13
Soule-Seabury House, 101
Specialty shops, 145-47
Sports, 69-73
Sportsman's Restaurant, 132
Spring Bull Studio, 142-43
Squash, 70
Star Clipper Dinner Train, 128-29
Statues, 55-57
Stevens House, 78
Stevens (John) House, 87
Stevens (Joseph) House, 88
Stevens Shop, 87
Stiles, Ezra, 79
Stiles House, 78-79
Surf's Up, 137
Synagogue, Touro, 37-38

Taxis, 21
Team One, 148, 159
Tennis, 69-70
   International Tennis Hall of Fame, 48-50
   pro, 68
Ternay, Admiral d'Arsac de, 40, 42
Thames Glass, 145
Theater, 138
Third Beach, 65

Index

Third & Elm Press, 146
Thomas Goddard House, 81
Tickets (dance music), 137
Tifobet, 138
Tilton House, 97
Tiverton and Sakonnet, 99-103
Topham House, 91
Topiary garden, 62
Tourism. See also Sightseeing
 clothing, 15-16
 getting oriented, 17-18
 getting to Newport, 16-17
 organized tours, 57-58
 seasons, 15
Tourist information, 161
Touro Cemetery, 38
Touro Synagogue, 37-38
Tours, 18
 organized, 57-58
 out of town, 98-109
 walking, 74-97
Townsend (Christopher) House and Studio, 90
Townsend (Gardner) House, 89
Townsend (Job) House, 90
Train to Newport, 17
Transportation
 in Newport, 20-21
 to Newport, 16-17
Trinity Church, 40-41, 83
Trist, 138
Trolleys, 21

United Baptist Church, 54
Upjohn, Richard, 26

Vanderbilt, Alva, 33
Vanderbilt, Cornelius, 29
Vernon House, 78
Victorian houses, walking tours, 92-97
Victorian Ladies, 115
Viewpoint, 143
Vikings, 39
Viking Tours, 57
Vineyards, 102
Vinland Wine Cellars, 147
Virginia Slims tennis tour, 68

Waldenbooks, 149
Walking, 18-19
Walking tours, 74-97
Wanton, Col. Joseph, Jr., 42
Wanton-Lyman-Hazard House, 43
Waring House, 95
Warren House, 91
Washington, George, 37
 statue of, 56
Washington Square, 75
Washington Square and Historic Hill, walking tour, 75-83
Watson Farm, 106
The Wave, 55
Whimsey Cottage, 118
Whitehall, 58-59
Whitehorne House, 51
White Horse Tavern, 85-86, 126
Whitestone, 95-96
Wilbour House (Little Compton), 102-3
Wilbour House (Newport), 81
Wilbur Ellery House, 79

Wilder House, 87
Wildlife, Norman Bird Sanctuary, 60
William Card House, 81
William Claggett House, 88-89
William Vareika Fine Arts, 142
Windsurfing, 71
Woodbine, 96
Wormeley House, 95

Yachting
    Classic Yacht Regatta, 69
    Museum of Yachting, 52-53
Yesterday's, 132-33

Also from The Countryman Press and Backcountry Publications

Countryman Press and Backcountry Publications, long known for fine books on travel and outdoor recreation, offer a range of practical and readable manuals. These carefully prepared books feature detailed trail or tour directions, notes on points of interest and natural highlights, maps and photographs.

Books about Rhode Island

Bird Walks in Rhode Island, $9.95
Canoeing Massachusetts, Rhode Island and Connecticut, $9.95
Walks & Rambles in Rhode Island, $9.95
More Walks & Rambles in Rhode Island, $9.95

Other Travel Guides

New England's Special Places, $12.95
Family Resorts of the Northeast, $12.95
Fifty Hikes in Connecticut, Third Edition $11.95
Fifty Hikes in Massachusetts, Second Edition $12.95
25 Mountain Bike Tours in Massachusetts, $9.95

This is only a sampling of our travel and outdoor recreation guides, available through bookstores and specialty shops. For a free catalog, write: The Countryman Press, Inc., Dept. APC, PO Box 175, Woodstock, VT 05091.